JERUSALEM

GENEVIEVE BELMAKER

Contents

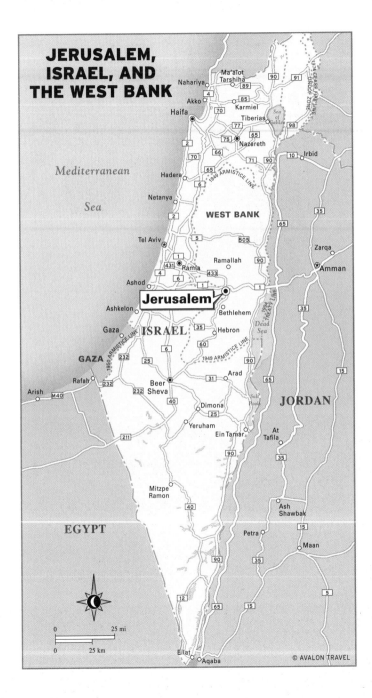

DISCOVER

Jerusalem

Calls to prayer echo out over valleys and rooftops. The ringing of church bells and the wailing siren for Shabbat are omnipresent. Deeply significant to the three largest monotheistic religions in the world—Judaism, Christianity, and Islam—the city of Jerusalem is filled with prayers and songs of different faiths. The timeworn, earthen-colored stones of the Old City have borne witness to thousands of years of history.

Pilgrims come here to walk in the footsteps that their religion took on its path to coming into the world: to touch the Western Wall, Judaism's holiest site; to stand where Jesus stood while crying over the coming destruction of Jerusalem; or to see the light gleaming off the golden Dome of the Rock, built over the stone where Muslims believe Muhammad ascended to heaven.

Many wait their entire lives to experience this timeless city, where the past feels present. See it yourself and you will begin to understand. Is it any wonder this place has inspired such passions, such devotion, such faith?

Clockwise from top left: bread vendor; prayer at the Western Wall; cat in a rug shop; the ceiling of the Church of the Holy Sepulchre; tile detail on the Dome of the Rock.

Planning Your Trip

Passports and Visas

Many countries have a **visa waiver agreement** with Israel, including the United States, Canada, and the United Kingdom, which means you only need to purchase a round-trip ticket to show your impending departure. You will be issued a **visa** upon entering Israel. Your **passport** must be good for at least six months past the date of your departure from the country.

Security

Check any travel advisories from foreign governments, such as the U.S. Department of State's travel advisories section on its website, before departing. Sporadic violence might mean that you choose not to visit a certain area.

Transportation

The best and most common way to get to this region is by airplane, which will take you to Tel Aviv's **Ben Gurion International Airport**. Entry from Jordan or Egypt is also possible by **car,** and arrival by **cruise ship** over international waters commonly occurs via the Port of Haifa.

Though the geographic area of Israel and the West Bank is fairly small, the complex security situation does require some advance planning. Within Jerusalem, **public transportation and taxis** make it fairly easy to get around. For travel beyond isolated locales, it is best to get a **rental car.** Long-distance **buses** will also get you around cheaply and efficiently, but they can require a sense of adventure and extra time for potential mishaps.

Tel Aviv's Ben Gurion International Airport

The **Israel Railways train** is also an option, especially for going to and from the airport.

What to Pack

Bringing the right clothing is incredibly important, particularly **comfortable shoes,** as there is a lot of rough terrain and bumpy cobblestones at various tourist sites, parks, and some cities. In some places you will be need to **dress conservatively,** particularly if you're a woman. A few long-sleeve shirts, pants, and long skirts should suffice. At least one cotton scarf to guard against dusty winds, chills, and sweat is a must for men and women. A scarf can be easily purchased once there, too.

Bring comfortable shoes to walk Jerusalem's cobblestone streets.

Stick to skirts that are either below the knee or more fitted, and lower-heeled or flat shoes, preferably with more support so you won't twist your ankle while walking on the uneven stones.

No matter when you go, take some kind of a **light jacket** (heavier in the winter months), as it can get cool in many areas during the evening. You will also need a **hat, sunglasses, sunscreen,** and a **good water canister** if you have one. Beyond that, you will just need a sense of adventure and a **good guidebook.**

the bus stop near the Western Wall

Jerusalem's Old City

Three Days in Jerusalem

This itinerary describes how to get a taste of the best of the city in three days, and it includes the major highlights and most popular sites.

Day 1

Have breakfast at your hotel and get an early start to the **Old City** to beat the heat and crowds. Take the most accessible entrance at the Jaffa Gate, and stop by the information center for any current happenings and available tours. From here you can also start to explore with a visit to either the **Rockefeller Archaeological Museum** or the **Tower of David Museum**.

Follow the main road downhill through the tightly packed shops selling all kinds of scarves, food, trinkets, jewelry, and souvenirs and try your hand at the regional custom of negotiating for a deal. Then head for the **Church of the Holy Sepulchre**, built on the spot where many believe Jesus was crucified, buried, and resurrected. From here, head to the **Austrian Hospice** for an incredible view of old and new Jerusalem from the rooftop and a piece of famous apple strudel in the quiet gardens.

After leaving the Austrian Hospice, wander around a bit as you work your way toward the **Western Wall, Al Aqsa Mosque,** and the **Dome of the Rock.** Pass the Western Wall and keep going toward the outer wall of the Old City, toward the **City of David** archaeological site. Here you can take a guided tour and walk through the ancient **Hezekiah's Tunnel,** knee-high in water. Skip the tunnel if you are claustrophobic, but if you're not, bring a flashlight.

Go back toward the Old City and take one of the many waiting taxis to dinner in City Center, preferably somewhere off of King David Street or in the popular pedestrian plaza and historic neighborhood of **Nahalat Shiva.**

Day 2

Take a taxi to the popular outdoor pedestrian shopping center **Mamilla,** where you can have breakfast alfresco at one of the restaurants with a vista of the new city and the landmark **Montefiore Windmill.** From Mamilla, it is a quick hop to the Old City, where you can check out anything you missed the previous day, such as the popular **Ramparts Walk tour** that circles the Old City along the top of the walls. Alternatively, there is the walk up the belfry tower at the **Church of the Redeemer** for one of the most highly rated and under-visited 360-degree views of the Old City.

Before it gets too late, exit the Old City through the Zion Gate and head up the hillside to **Mount Zion,** where some believe that Jesus held the Last Supper and King David's Tomb can be found. Don't let anybody talk you into making a "donation" here; the site is free. At Mount Zion you will also find the lovely **Dormition Abbey** and great vistas of the city from multiple vantage points.

Take a taxi to the top of the **Mount of Olives,** where you will see the view of the Old City of Jerusalem that Jesus is said to have shed tears over when telling of its coming destruction. Go by foot into the nearby Arab village and have lunch at one of the many small restaurants serving Arab food before heading back down the hillside by taxi. Ask to be dropped off at the **Church of the Pater Noster,** and then walk downhill to the nearby **Dome and Chapel of the Ascension** and the **Garden of Gethsemane.**

From the Garden of Gethsemane, it is a long walk or a quick taxi ride to a City Center restaurant; try something near Tolerance Square this time.

Dormition Abbey

Bible Lands Museum

Day 3

Enjoy breakfast at your hotel before heading out to see some of Jerusalem's museums. Go by bus or taxi to **The Israel Museum,** about 20 minutes west of the Old City by car. Allow at least a half day to explore the museum and its rich, famed exhibits specializing in Judaica and Jewish history as well as regional history. Take advantage of the museum's restaurant for lunch and hop across the street to the **Bible Lands Museum.** Then take a taxi to the nearby and underrated **Monastery of the Cross,** located in the valley where the wood for Jesus's cross is said to have been taken from. From here take another taxi to **Yad Vashem** Holocaust memorial, or walk five minutes to the bus that will take you to the light-rail. The light-rail will deliver you to **Mount Herzl** and the associated Herzl museum, near the

spices for sale in Machane Yehuda Market

shuttle buses that take you down Yad Vashem's long drive. Allow at least four hours and some time for food or a cold drink at the cafeteria where you can meditate on the sweeping view of the Jerusalem forest.

From Yad Vashem, take the light-rail train to City Center and the famous **Machane Yehuda Market** (the *shuk*), where you can wander around and finish with dinner in one of the *shuk*'s many wonderful restaurants or cafés. In the evening, the *shuk*'s nightlife cranks up, and the quiet pubs turn into hopping parties, some with live music.

Six Days in Jerusalem

This section maps out a travel strategy with an emphasis on archaeological sites alongside new attractions and places to eat and play. Think **ancient archaeological sites** in and around the Old City by day, and **rooftop drinks and food** overlooking the city or live music by night. It also includes a few notable places in the vicinity of Jerusalem. The time frame is divided based on the days of the week, due to Jerusalem's limited access during Shabbat (Fri.-Sat. night).

Day 1: Sunday

After a good night's sleep at your hotel, put on your most comfortable shoes and get ready for some serious walking in the **Old City.** Start from the information center at the Jaffa Gate, and pick a couple of key points in the Old City to explore, but allow for plenty of time to wander, take photos, and bargain for deals.

From the Jaffa Gate, you can easily explore the **Armenian Quarter** (mostly residential) and loop back up to the **Jewish Quarter** and the old Roman **Cardo,** which includes some high-end shopping. Keep going north to the **Christian Quarter** and you can see a number of churches, including the **Church of the Holy Sepulchre.** Head back out to the foot of the Jaffa Gate where you can take in the air-conditioned shops and bookstores at modern and upscale **Mamilla,** and have lunch and a coffee.

the Armenian Quarter

Walk from Mamilla to **Nahalat Shiva,** where you can spend a couple of leisurely hours exploring the shops full of handmade crafts, before you walk to the **Jerusalem Time Elevator** exhibit for an interactive trip through Jerusalem history. Stay in Nahalat Shiva for dinner to experience one of Jerusalem's most famous and authentically Middle Eastern restaurants, **Tmol Shilshom.**

Day 2: Monday

After a leisurely breakfast, get a picnic lunch and head to **The Israel Museum** by taxi or bus for a late morning viewing session of antiquities and Jewish and regional history and art, including the Shrine of the Book, which houses the Dead Sea Scrolls. Directly across the way is the **Bible Lands Museum,** with its gorgeous ancient jewelry displays and emphasis on biblical history.

When you've had enough air-conditioning, take a quick taxi ride or a 25-minute walk to a free tour of the **Supreme Court of Israel;** the tour starts at noon and then just hop over to the **Knesset (Israeli Parliament)** for another free tour, starting at 2pm, if you have time. Stop in the **Wohl Rose Garden** with its vast collection of roses on a gently sloping lawn overlooking Jerusalem for your picnic lunch. The roses will stay in full bloom late into the year, and after lunch you can explore the grounds and the approximately 400 varieties of roses.

Head back to your hotel by taxi and rest up before dinner at any one of the City Center restaurants near Tolerance Square. After dinner, take a stroll through **Tolerance Square** with its lively evening atmosphere including street musicians, and get dessert from one of the ice cream shops.

monks leaving the Church of the Holy Sepulchre in the Christian Quarter

Day 3: Tuesday

Make sure you are conservatively dressed or have something to cover your shoulders and legs, but with pants that can be rolled up, and head back to the **Old City** in the morning (bring a flashlight). Take a taxi to the Damascus Gate in East Jerusalem, and enter the Old City through the gate to explore the **Muslim Quarter** and see some of the stations along the **Via Dolorosa,** where Jesus carried his cross on his way to be crucified. Continue along the Via Dolorosa to the northern side of the **Dome of the Rock, Al Aqsa Mosque,** and the **Western Wall,** holy sites to Christians, Muslims, and Jews. Just before the entrance to the Western Wall there are a number of restaurants where you can get lunch and rest before continuing.

Exit the Old City just past the Western Wall and you'll be in the East Jerusalem neighborhood of **Silwan,** where the **City of David** is located. Make sure you buy a ticket that includes a trip through **Hezekiah's Tunnel** (a good activity when the midday sun is out). After traipsing through the 2,700-year-old tunnel for 580 yards to the **Pool of Siloam** and touring the City of David, take a rest back at your hotel and freshen up for the evening.

Before dinner, take in the sunset at the swanky Mamilla Hotel's rooftop terrace bar and restaurant (make reservations in advance). You can stay for dinner after enjoying the view of the old and new cities, or head downstairs to try one of Mamilla's restaurants.

Day 4: Wednesday

Set out early to the **Mount of Olives** for an awe-inspiring sunrise. Get a taxi to take you to the top of the Mount of Olives' highest vista point, above the old Jewish Cemetery, right next to the Seven Arches Hotel. From here,

Station 9 on the Via Dolorosa

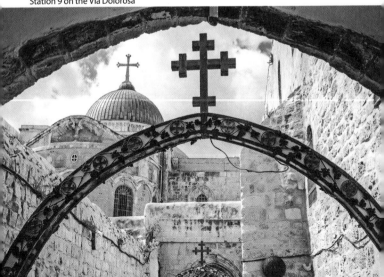

enjoy the incredible view of old and new Jerusalem. Walk down the hill and go through the **Jewish Cemetery,** or just continue downhill to various vista points for photos. Continue downhill toward the Old City, stopping to peek inside the churches along the way. It's a long walk, but frequented by taxis if you get tired.

Take a taxi to **Mount Zion** just outside the Zion Gate at the Old City, and explore **Dormition Abbey** and the area near **King David's Tomb.**

For lunch, hop on the light-rail train bound for the **Machane Yehuda Market** (the *shuk*) where you can explore the massive array of stalls with its fresh produce, spices, and regional sweets and snacks. Stop off at one of the *shuk*'s many restaurants for lunch. From here, catch the light-rail train to **Yad Vashem** and **Mount Herzl.** Start with Yad Vashem, which can take several hours (children under the age of 10 are not allowed in the main hall).

Head back out just before dark if you have the energy to the Old City for the **Night Spectacular** light show at the Tower of David Museum citadel at the Jaffa Gate.

Day 5: Thursday

Use Thursday to visit the **Museum on the Seam** for a detailed and clear-eyed look at the juxtaposition of East and West Jerusalem. Go by taxi to the **L.A. Mayer Museum for Islamic Art** and then take a 15-minute walk downhill to the historic **German Colony** neighborhood either for a guided tour (arranged in advance) of the beautiful, Templar-style buildings and homes or to do some shopping for essentials or souvenirs along popular Emek Refaim Street.

looking up at Yad Vashem's Hall of Names

Pilgrimage Sites

prayer in the women's section of the Western Wall

It isn't known as the Holy Land for nothing. Here is a list of some of the most important religious and spiritual sites in Jerusalem.

- **Al Aqsa Mosque next to the Dome of the Rock** is the third holiest site in the Muslim world (Muslim Quarter, Old City).

- **Church of the Holy Sepulchre** is widely recognized as the site of the crucifixion and resurrection of Jesus (Christian Quarter, Old City).

- **Mount of Olives** is the site of many miraculous occurrences and an extremely significant location in Judaism, Christianity, and Islam (near the Old City).

- **Mount Zion** is one possible site of the Last Supper and the locale of King David's Tomb (near the Old City).

- **Western Wall** is a remnant of the western wall of the destroyed Second Temple. It is a popular destination for prayer by Jews and sometimes the site of large-scale religious events (Jewish Quarter, Old City).

pilgrims visiting Al Aqsa Mosque

For lunch, walk 10 minutes to the popular **First Station** train station culinary and shopping complex, built from the foundation of Jerusalem's former main train station, which is more than 120 years old. There is more shopping to be had here in a lively atmosphere that often includes musical performances. Follow the adjacent trails in **Train Track Park** north to hilly **Bloomfield Garden** with its beautiful fountain and pathways. Walk through the park until you reach the **Montefiore Windmill** and its sweeping vista point of East Jerusalem and the separation barrier in the distance. Continue on to the **King David Hotel** and the YMCA, both with historic architecture and idyllic outdoor seating for dinner.

Day 6: Friday

Friday in Jerusalem tends to be a bit frenzied as locals take care of last-minute shopping before the city shuts down for 24 hours. It is a good day to go back to the Old City's **Rockefeller Archaeological Museum** to see antiquities or take the **Ramparts Walk** along the top of the wall surrounding the Old City in the morning. A short taxi ride away, at the top of King David Street you will find the Bezalel Art Academy, where the **Bezalel Art Fair** with 150 local vendors selling locally made arts, crafts, and food is held. It is the perfect spot for souvenir shopping. There are numerous restaurants nearby for lunch, but plan to wrap things up by about 2pm.

For a quiet dinner and wine with a rooftop view of the city, go by taxi to the imposing Pontifical Institute Notre Dame's four-star **Roof Top Wine and Cheese Restaurant**.

the Montefiore Windmill

Jerusalem

Look for ★ to find recommended sights, activities, dining, and lodging.

Highlights

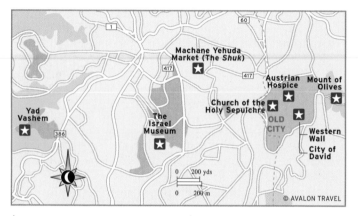

© AVALON TRAVEL

★ **Church of the Holy Sepulchre:** One of the most important sites for Christians in Jerusalem, this is where Jesus is believed to have been crucified (page 31).

★ **Austrian Hospice:** Hidden from most tourists by a nondescript outer wall, this oasis in the Old City offers respite and an amazing vista (page 33).

★ **Western Wall:** The most important site in Judaism, the Western Wall, also known as the Kotel, is situated in the southeastern corner of the Old City (page 35).

★ **Mount of Olives:** One of the most dramatic views of Jerusalem exists alongside numerous important religious and historic sites (page 42).

★ **City of David:** Play archaeologist by wading through an ancient aqueduct or sifting through ancient dirt (page 45).

★ **The Israel Museum:** The museum's rich, detailed exhibits on Jewish history, archaeology, and regional treasures are a must-see (page 47).

★ **Yad Vashem:** The largest Holocaust museum in the world is a solemn pilgrimage (page 50).

★ **Machane Yehuda Market (The Shuk):** The outdoor market near City Center is frequented by locals of all ages and practically a required experience for visitors (page 62).

The region's religious, histori-cal, and political center, Jeru-salem is a heady mix of striking architecture, distinct regional cuisine, and compelling tourist attractions.

Jerusalem is also increasingly a center for entertainment and diversion, entrepreneurship, and innovation.

Most people start their time in Jerusalem by exploring some of the thousands of years of epic history contained within the Ottoman-era walls of the Old City. This is also where great shopping, entertainment, guided tours and cultural activities can be found among the four distinct, but overlapping quarters: Muslim, Jewish, Christian, and Armenian. The massive Western Wall and the Dome of the Rock in the background by day and the Tower of David light show by night are must-sees. Plus, nowhere else in the city is bargaining with vendors for a souvenir trinket or scarf quite as fun.

Within an easy distance of the Old City are numerous important churches, synagogues, and other holy sites, many of which can be found along the walk up the hill to the Mount of Olives with its breathtaking view of the city and the important Jewish cemetery below.

Jerusalem also boasts an outstanding offering of restaurants and entertainment, regionally made goods, and world-class museums, parks, and gardens. Any number of restaurants in City Center won't disappoint, and there is no better way to experience the famous soft evening air of Jerusalem than at a sidewalk café with a rich cappuccino, possibly after a trip through the maze of the famed market (the *shuk*). Of the city's many beautiful parks, Wohl Rose Garden's hundreds of roses and rolling hills make for a serene place for a picnic and stroll. It is also within walking distance of a tour of parliament. Just a taxi ride away is the Israel Museum and the Bible

Previous: the Dome of the Rock; the Western Wall. **Above:** mosaic in the Church of the Holy Sepulchre.

Lands Museum with their rich displays of regional history and of course the world-renowned Yad Vashem Holocaust Memorial.

When too much history and culture start to overwhelm, the light atmosphere of First Station in West Jerusalem with its dining, shopping, and entertainment is a great diversion. There are even nearby movie theaters at Cinema City and the Jerusalem Cinematheque with features in English or foreign-language movies with English subtitles. It's all there for the taking.

ORIENTATION

Jerusalem is a very ancient and complex city that has more than 2,000 major and minor archaeological sites. Most visitors explore the city by starting with major tourist spots that include the **Old City, Yad Vashem, Machane Yehuda Market**, the **Western Wall**, and **City Center**.

The Old City

The Old City is an unforgettable experience that is quintessential Jerusalem. You could easily spend days exploring layers of history from thousands of years.

The Old City is divided into four quarters that date back to Roman times: the **Muslim Quarter**, the **Christian Quarter**, the **Armenian Quarter**, and the **Jewish Quarter**. Each quarter has many **free sights** worth a visit, and there are seemingly endless rows of **ancient shops,** selling everything from scarves to antiquities.

Many people follow the **Via Dolorosa,** believed to be the last steps of Jesus on his way to be crucified. The route has 14 stations of historical significance and is rich with additional history that came well after Jesus's time. Following the Via Dolorosa is a good way to learn some of the Old City's story. Free audio guides, pamphlets, and group tours are available.

City Center

Jerusalem's City Center is vibrant, though a bit touristy, and boasts excellent restaurants and sidewalk cafés, shopping, and some entertainment. At the west side of City Center is the renowned **Machane Yehuda Market** (the *shuk*). City Center is bordered on the west by King George Street until it turns into Agripas Street in the north and meets with Agron Street on the south. It is bordered on the east by Shivtet Israel Street and on the north by Hanevi'im Street.

The highlights of Jerusalem **nightlife** are found in City Center, including live music venues, street music, pubs, wine bars, clubs, restaurants, and cafés that stay open into the wee hours. There are also a couple of good **museums,** numerous **hotels,** and some of the best **shopping** in town. It's the most convenient place to go for anything you need during your travels, from electric converters to toiletries to money-changing.

East Jerusalem

Once you cross the (now invisible) line between East and West Jerusalem,

Jerusalem

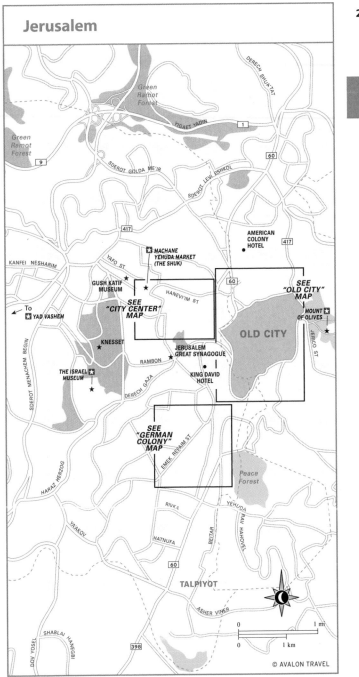

© AVALON TRAVEL

City Center

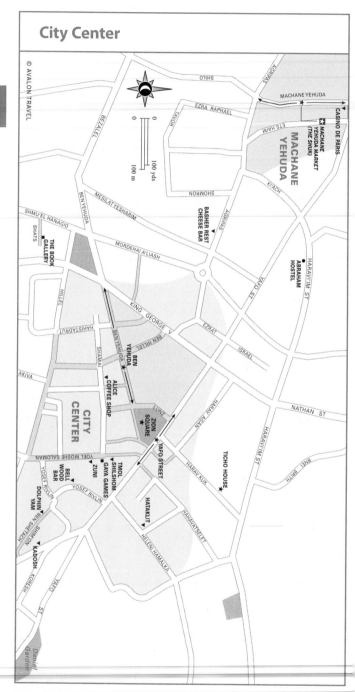

© AVALON TRAVEL

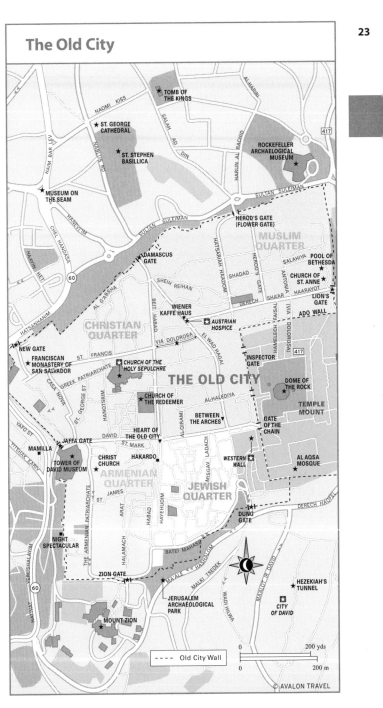

The Old City

Landmarks and sites:

- TOMB OF THE KINGS
- ST. GEORGE CATHEDRAL
- ST. STEPHEN BASILLICA
- ROCKEFELLER ARCHAEOLOGICAL MUSEUM
- MUSEUM ON THE SEAM
- HEROD'S GATE (FLOWER GATE)
- DAMASCUS GATE
- POOL OF BETHESDA
- CHURCH OF ST. ANNE
- LION'S GATE
- WIENER KAFFE HAUS
- AUSTRIAN HOSPICE
- NEW GATE
- FRANCISCAN MONASTERY OF SAN SALVADOR
- CHURCH OF THE HOLY SEPULCHRE
- INSPECTOR GATE
- DOME OF THE ROCK
- CHURCH OF THE REDEEMER
- BETWEEN THE ARCHES
- TEMPLE MOUNT
- GATE OF THE CHAIN
- HEART OF THE OLD CITY
- JAFFA GATE
- MAMILLA
- CHRIST CHURCH
- HAKARDO
- WESTERN WALL
- AL AQSA MOSQUE
- TOWER OF DAVID MUSEUM
- NIGHT SPECTACULAR
- DUNG GATE
- ZION GATE
- JERUSALEM ARCHAEOLOGICAL PARK
- HEZEKIAH'S TUNNEL
- CITY OF DAVID
- MOUNT ZION

Quarters:

- MUSLIM QUARTER
- CHRISTIAN QUARTER
- THE OLD CITY
- ARMENIAN QUARTER
- JEWISH QUARTER

Legend:

- - - - Old City Wall

0   200 yds
0   200 m

© AVALON TRAVEL

The First and Second Temples

No visitor to Jerusalem can escape references to the First Temple and the Second Temple, recalling historical time periods when two different massive Jewish temples stood approximately where Al Aqsa Mosque is now located. Both temples were destroyed, and the main remnant is the outer western wall of the Second Temple courtyard, where people flock from all over the world to pray (known as the Wailing Wall, the Kotel, or the Western Wall).

According to Jewish traditions, both temples were destroyed on the 9th of Av on the Jewish calendar. Every year, those destructions are marked by the day of mourning called Tisha B'av. There are several other tragic disasters in Jewish history associated with Tisha B'av. But, because of its relation to the destruction of the temples, the plaza of the Western Wall is filled with throngs of Jewish mourners every Tisha B'av (in August).

During the **First Temple period** (1200-586 BC), the First Temple was built in 1000 BC by King Solomon after King David had conquered Jerusalem and made it his capital. The Temple was destroyed in 586 BC by Nebuchadnezzar, the king of Babylon, when he conquered Jerusalem. There are scant remains of the temple on the south hill of the City of David. Evidence of the conquering and destruction of the city can be found in the Burnt House and the House of the Bullae.

From the First Temple period there are significant remains of preparations made by King Hezekiah when a siege on the city by the Assyrian king Sennacherib was imminent in 701 BC. Those remains include Hezekiah's Tunnel and the Broad Wall in the Jewish Quarter.

The beginning of the **Second Temple period** (586 BC-AD 70) is marked by the return of Jews to Jerusalem from their exile in Babylon in 538 BC. They were allowed to return under an edict issued by Cyrus, king of Persia. By 515 BC the reinstated Jewish residents had completed building the Second Temple.

The time of the Second Temple and subsequent ages after its destruction are divided into different periods: the **Persian period** (586-332 BC), the **Hellenistic period** (332-63 BC), and the **Roman period** (63 BC-AD 324). In 37 BC, King Herod enlarged the Temple Mount and rebuilt the temple with the consent of the public. During the Roman period, in AD 70, the Second Temple was destroyed, along with all of Jerusalem, by Titus's army. It was also during this period that Jesus was in Jerusalem. He was crucified about 40 years before the destruction of the city.

Significant archaeological remains from the Second Temple period, including the Kidron Valley tombs, the Western Wall, Robinson's Arch, the Herodian residential quarter, numerous other tombs, and walls can be visited today.

BCE (Before Common Era) and CE (Common Era) are used throughout Israel and are numerically equivalent to BC and AD, respectively.

there is a palpable sense of stepping into a different culture due to East Jerusalem's largely Arab population.

East Jerusalem has a good selection of affordable **hotels, shopping** options on Salah al-Din Street, and a wide variety of **Arab and Persian food** from Lebanon, Syria, Iraq, Iran, and Turkey.

Because of the Arab cultural and religious stigma against drinking,

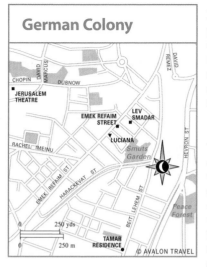

East Jerusalem is not the best place to have a night out with a few beers and music. Many restaurants do offer the traditional *nargila* (water pipe) that can be smoked with a menu of flavored tobacco after a meal.

West Jerusalem

West Jerusalem consists of several distinctive neighborhoods where visitors tend to spend much time. A popular area for shopping and dining is the German Colony encompassed by the triangle formed by Emek Refaim Street, Yehuda Street, and Hebron Road. The area at the northern tip of the triangle, known as Yemin Moshe-Mishkenot Sha'ananim, is surrounded by parks and has nearby family-friendly entertainment.

Originally settled by German Templars, the German Colony's Emek Refaim Street is popular with tourists and locals for its hip and diverse selection of restaurants, set against a very distinct backdrop of older homes. The general area also features museums and theaters that are within walking distance or a short cab ride of each other. They range from Islamic art to regional historical artifacts to contemporary film and a little bit in between.

West Jerusalem is home to the Israel Museum, the Bible Lands Museum, the future site of the National Campus for the Archaeology of Israel, and several others.

PLANNING YOUR TIME

Jerusalem's terrain and sights are layered and complex. That makes for an interesting visit but presents a challenge in terms of seeing the major highlights of the city in fewer than three days. Six days allow you to comfortably visit all of the best sights as well as enjoy some of the local culture, cuisine, and make a few day trips to nearby spots.

When to Go

There are two major considerations when planning a visit to Jerusalem: the weather and the holiday calendar. The climate is inviting. In the summer months, the average temperature typically goes above 80-90°F daily, but when the sun goes down, pleasant, cool, breezy evenings in the mid-70s are the norm.

The best time of year to visit is May-July. August-September is very hot

Jerusalem's Conquerors

The list of those who have conquered, occupied, or destroyed Jerusalem is lengthy:

- King David conquers Jerusalem in 1000 BC.

- Nebuchadnezzar, king of Babylon, conquers Jerusalem and destroys the First Temple in 586 BC.

- Alexander the Great conquers Jerusalem in 332 BC.

- Antiochus III conquers Jerusalem in 200 BC.

- Pompeius conquers Jerusalem in 63 BC and Roman rule begins.

- Herod occupies Jerusalem and fortifies significant public buildings.

- Titus's army destroys Jerusalem and the Second Temple in AD 70.

- Transjordan captures East Jerusalem in 1948.

- Israel retakes East Jerusalem and reunifies the city in 1967.

but bearable weather-wise, but could prove very tricky logistically. For three weeks in August, the Jewish orthodox community has a major vacation season, and they flood nearly every corner of the city's museums and parks. At the end of August, the Muslim community of the city finishes their holy month of fasting for Ramadan and come out to enjoy the end of summer in the parks. During August, it is not uncommon to see popular gathering places like Gan Sacher Park overflowing with families cooking out and playing in fountains. Other major Jewish holidays of Yom Kippur and Sukkot usually fall in September (check the Jewish calendar, which changes by the year).

Getting Around

Jerusalem is an ancient city that can be tricky to maneuver in if you take a wrong turn, especially when traveling by car. It's highly recommended to go by foot or take advantage of Jerusalem's efficient bus system, ample taxis, and the light-rail train to get around.

Navigating Jerusalem is fairly easy if you have a clear idea of how much time and money you want to spend. Taxicabs are everywhere but cost 25 percent more on weekends between 9pm and 5am. There is a discounted public transportation ticket for tourists for access to both the light-rail and the public buses. However, the light-rail stops are fairly limited and the bus system, while convenient once you get the hang of it, can be tricky. There is also a double-decker city tour bus that you can hop on and off all day long at major sights with the purchase of a 24- or 48-hour ticket.

Jerusalem's history, like the city itself, is winding, confusing, and full of unexpected twists and turns. For millennia, it has been a religious center for peoples of three major faiths: Jews, Christians, and Muslims. It has endured as a flashpoint of religious, ethnic, and geopolitical tension through to modern times.

In ancient times, Jerusalem was mainly confined to the area now known as the Old City, contained within the walls that offered protection from attackers, invaders, and the elements. The city has been conquered, destroyed, and rebuilt more than once. In fact, it has long been an object of pursuit for ambitious rulers and empires. The first evidence of human life in Jerusalem is around 4500 BC. The first reference to the name Jerusalem (Urushalimum) was in 1500 BC.

In modern times, largely since the return of the Jewish Diaspora to Israel, there have been raging battles and political debates over who controls and has a claim on the holy city.

In 1948, soldiers from Transjordan's Arab Legion (which became the Hashemite Kingdom of Jordan in 1949) tried to capture the entire city during the War of Independence. But Israeli fighters were able to defend significant portions of the western part of the city. After the Arab Legion destroyed the Jewish Quarter of the Old City and expelled the residents, a cease-fire agreement was signed. Outside of the walls was known as the New City and mostly Israeli-controlled.

In April 1949, an armistice agreement was signed along the 1948 cease-fire line between Israeli and Transjordan forces. The line between east and west was divided by barbed wire, concrete walls, minefields, and bunkers. East Jerusalem, including holy sites, was occupied by Transjordan and West Jerusalem became the capital of Israel.

In 1967, the Israeli Defense Force (or IDF) battled again with Jordan and took control of East Jerusalem. The city was reunified under Israeli control, with a promise that religious sites for all faiths would be protected. For Jews this meant that they gained access to Temple Mount and the Western Wall and could freely visit and pray at these sites.

Today you can still see the dividing line between East and West Jerusalem. If you stand along the route taken by the light-rail train near the Old City, you can imagine a now-invisible line that used to be there. The east side of Jerusalem is a bit more ramshackle, the roads aren't well maintained in many places, and the architecture is more distinctly Arab. The west side of Jerusalem is more upscale and most residents are Jewish.

Tensions between East and West Jerusalem are ongoing but typically take on more subtle and political forms, though sometimes there is violence. The Arab neighborhood of Silwan is a stark example. Under court order, many Arab residents there have been told that their homes do not legally belong to them and have been forced out. Violence between Arabs and Israelis sometimes erupts in the area with Israelis firing rubber bullets and Arabs throwing stones and burning large trash cans.

You could spend days on end sightseeing in Jerusalem and never run out of interesting things to look at, experience, and learn about. This is especially true for those who have a love of history, archaeology, and spirituality. It is one of the most overwhelming cities in the world; for all the mysteries you discover, there are always a dozen more you have yet to learn.

Many of Jerusalem's major sights are centered on the Old City and the nearby Mount of Olives and Mount Zion. The Old City is the heart of Jerusalem, and includes major sights such as the Western Wall, the Dome of the Rock, the Church of the Holy Sepulchre, the Via Dolorosa, and many, many more. The Mount of Olives is also layered with sights significant to Christians, Muslims, and Jews. Not far from the Old City, the city becomes more residential and moves with the rhythm of its residents, who live in and around important museums, well-known parks, the world-famous Machane Yehuda Market, and the compound of the national government of Israel.

The trick to sightseeing in Jerusalem is to measure how much any particular endeavor might cost in money and energy, especially in the scorching hot summer months. There are no special combination tourism tickets, and the sights that have entrance fees range on average NIS20-50 per person, sometimes more. Some sights that seem fascinating and worth paying the entrance fee for are run by organizations that have a political or religious agenda, and you might be held captive to a monologue about it during your tour.

Many museums have an open late day of the week or windows of limited free admission. In fact, many of the best things to do and see in Jerusalem are free or cost very little.

THE OLD CITY
Via Dolorosa

One of the most revered sites among Christian pilgrims visiting Jerusalem is the **Via Dolorosa** (Way of Sorrows), the path that Jesus is said to have walked on his way to his crucifixion almost 2,000 years ago. Along the path, fourteen numbered "stations" mark locations of significant moments during Jesus's journey as he bore the cross he was to be crucified upon. The Via Dolorosa begins just inside the Lion's Gate in the Muslim Quarter and ends in the Christian Quarter inside the Church of the Holy Sepulchre, where the last five stations are located. Pilgrims frequently kneel in prayer at the stations, which are points along the street marked with Roman numerals. Much of the Via Dolorosa is accessible 24 hours, and the entire route is free. The Via Dolorosa is part of the living history of the Old City, and the stories connected to it have been passed down through the generations and thus more based in tradition than accurate history.

It is recommended to visit the Via Dolorosa with a guided tour or join the **Via Dolorosa procession** led by Franciscans friars on Fridays from Station 1 (3pm Oct.-Mar., 4pm Apr.-Nov., El Omariye School just inside the Lion's Gate, free). Check with the **Christian Information Centre** in the Old City (Omar Ibn el-Khattab Square at Jaffa Gate, www.cicts.org, 9am-5:30pm Mon.-Fri. and 9am-12:30pm Sat.). As with many other sights, maps, audio tours, and video are available on the **Old City's official website** (www.jerusalem.old-city.org.il). A free MP3 audio file and map of the trail from the Jerusalem Development Authority can be downloaded from the website.

STATION 1

Just inside the Lion's Gate in front of El Omariye School is a round, black seal imprinted with the Roman numeral I on an outer wall. The station is where Pontius Pilate condemned Jesus to death. The station is located at the northwest corner of Temple Mount.

STATION 2

Across the street is the Roman numeral II. Here Jesus was given his cross, whipped, and mockingly dressed in a robe and given a crown of thorns by Roman soldiers. The compound includes the Roman Catholic Church of the Condemnation and the Convent of the Flagellation.

STATION 3

The corner of Via Dolorosa and El Wad (Hagai) Street marks where Jesus fell under the weight of the cross for the first time. The route then traces the western side of the Temple Mount. The Polish Catholic church, the Austrian Hospice, and a 15th-century chapel are nearby.

STATION 4

On El Wad Street is the Roman numeral IV at Our Church of the Lady of the Sun, where Jesus is believed to have encountered his mother, Mary. The Armenian church is home to a 5th-century floor and two sandal footprints said to belong to Mary.

STATION 5

At the corner of El Wad Street is the Roman numeral V and a small Franciscan church built in 1229 to mark the location where Simon bore the cross for Jesus. An old square stone to the right of the door of the church is believed to bear the handprint of Jesus.

STATION 6

Midway down Via Dolorosa just before Souq Khan al-Zeit Street (the market street) is the Roman numeral VI and Our Church of the Holy Face with its restored Crusader arches. This is the station where a woman named Veronica wiped the face of Jesus.

STATION 7

At the intersection of Souq Khan al-Zeit Street and Via Dolorosa is the Roman numeral VII, marking where Jesus fell for the second time. Behind the black doors is a small chapel. Just beyond a massive Roman column is the Chapel of the Seventh Station.

STATION 8

The Roman numeral VIII is at Aqabat al-Khanqah across from the Station VIII Souvenir bazaar. The station is marked by a stone embedded in the wall of the Monastery of St. Charalampos bearing the engraving IC-XC NI-KA, which means "Jesus Christ conquers." This is where Jesus spoke to the women of Jerusalem and told them not to weep for him, but for themselves and their children.

STATION 9

A zigzag route down Souq Khan al-Zeit Street and up 28 stone steps leads to Station IX with its cross painted on a stone pillar next to an archway where Jesus fell for the third time. Adjacent to the Church of the Holy Sepulchre, the route here winds around the building of the Coptic Patriarchate. Nearby is the Ethiopian Church of St. Michael and a Coptic church with paintings that depict scenes from the Bible.

STATION 10

At the southern end of Souq Khan al-Zeit Street to the right is Souq al-Dabbagha. Cross the courtyard to the entrance of the Church of the Holy Sepulchre, where the last five stations are located. Start at Station X, the Chapel of the Franks, where Jesus was stripped of his clothes.

the Seventh Station of the Cross on the Via Dolorosa

Station XI is the interior of the Church of the Holy Sepulchre where Jesus
was nailed to the cross.

STATION 12

A Greek Orthodox crucifixion altar inside the church marks Station XII
in the Church of the Holy Sepulchre where Jesus was crucified and died
on the cross. A silver disk with a central hole under the altar marks where
the cross stood. Pilgrims kneel and kiss the spot.

STATION 13

A large stone marks Station XIII in the Church of the Holy Sepulchre where
the body of Jesus is said to have been laid and prepared for burial after he
died. The station is encased and has an open top for pilgrims to touch.

STATION 14

The tomb of Jesus and the final station of the Via Dolorosa is located in the
rotunda inside a small inner chamber past the Chapel of the Angel in the
Church of the Holy Sepulchre. A marble lid covers the tomb.

The Christian Quarter
ST. SAVIOR CHURCH (FRANCISCAN
MONASTERY OF SAN SALVADOR)

Just inside the New Gate you will find the **Franciscan Monastery of San
Salvador,** also known as **St. Savior Church** (1 St. Francis St., tel. 02/626-
6595, http://catholicchurch-holyland.com, 8am-5pm daily, free). The visit
of St. Francis of Assisi to the Holy Land in 1219 marked the beginning of
the Franciscan monks following in his footsteps, and to this day the San
Salvador Monastery in the Old City is the center of the Franciscan Order
in the Holy Land and the Middle East.

The monastery, which visitors cannot enter, does have a church that
is free to go into with a magnificent vaulted ceiling and pipe organ.
Construction on the church was completed in the 19th century.

You might see members of the Franciscan Order while walking about
the Old City. They are distinguishable by their simple, brown robes with
a rope belt knotted three times in honor of the vows of their order: obedi-
ence, poverty, and chastity.

★ CHURCH OF THE HOLY SEPULCHRE

One of the most popular destinations in the Old City, the **Church of the
Holy Sepulchre** (Suq Khan e-Zeit and Christian Quarter Rd., tel. 02/627-
3314, www.holysepulchre.com, 5am-8pm daily Apr.-Sept., 5am-7pm daily
Oct.-Mar., free) is the most important site for Christians in the world. Also
known as the Church of the Resurrection, the dark, cavernous structure
houses four stations of the Via Dolorosa and is thus constantly filled with
throngs of pilgrims.

Just past the church's massive outdoor courtyard is the end of the Via Dolorosa. At the entrance is the Chapel of the Franks, and the looming interior includes a Greek Orthodox crucifixion altar where Jesus is said to have been crucified. A large stone (stone of unction) to the left is the place where, according to tradition, the body of Jesus was prepared for burial. In the rotunda inside a small inner chamber, past the Chapel of the Angel, is a marble encased tomb said to be the place where Jesus was buried. A massive vaulted dome rises above the tomb with a center of light that streams downward.

The church was one of many commissioned by Constantine the Great after he converted to Christianity. Work on the church began in AD 326, and some historians believe that Constantine's builders dug around the tomb of Jesus. Since then, it has suffered tremendous neglect, desecration, and damage as the city has changed hands and rulers. The current church is the result of the joint efforts of the Latin, Greek, and Armenian communities who banded together in 1959 for a major restoration project. All that could be preserved in the process was, but the current condition of the church is a mixture of Byzantine, Crusader, medieval, and modern styles. Control of the church is also divided among different denominations of Christians.

CHURCH OF THE REDEEMER

The Lutheran **Church of the Redeemer** (24 Muristan Rd., tel. 02/627-1111, www.elcjhl.org, 9am-1pm and 1:30pm-5pm Mon.-Sat., NIS10) is easy to spot with its distinctive bell tower that can be reached by trekking up almost 200 steps. The church's interior walls are made of simple and relatively

the Church of the Holy Sepulchre

unadorned white stone with massive arches. The church was built by Kaiser Wilhelm in the late 1800s, and he later brought his wife with him to personally dedicate it in 1898. He was the first Western ruler to visit Jerusalem and infamously ordered the door of Jaffa Gate to be removed so he could enter the Old City unimpeded while riding his horse wearing a tall, spiked helmet. The gate was never repaired and is the only entrance point in the Old City without full gate.

The church is home to Lutheran congregations that speak Arabic, German, English, and Danish, and it is the site of frequent musical performances.

★ AUSTRIAN HOSPICE

In order to find the **Austrian Hospice** (37 Via Dolorosa, near Damascus Gate, tel. 02/626-5800, www.austrianhospice.com, 24 hours daily, free) you will have to ask merchants for directions because it is extremely well hidden.

You could easily pass by this gem in the Old City without knowing it is here. Behind a very nondescript set of double doors is one of the most serene spots in the Old City. Ring the bell outside and you will be buzzed in to an inner gate. The location was chosen by Austria's first consul general as a place to build (and establish a local presence) in Jerusalem and was opened as a pilgrims' house in 1856. The hospice functions as a high-end hotel, and visitors can wander the hallways filled with photographs of the Holy Land.

There are two points here not to miss: the garden café with its famed apple strudel and the spectacular rooftop view of the Old City and the Dome of the Rock. You can reach the roof by taking the elevator and then the stairs. Once on the roof, you can enjoy the view from a bench, and take your time to absorb the awesome sight of the Old City. You can also take as long as you like at one of the many outdoor tables in the garden near the entrance (which is elevated two stories above street level) for a quiet coffee, beer, or snack.

the courtyard at the Austrian Hospice

The Muslim Quarter
CHURCH OF ST. ANNE

Near the beginning of the Via Dolorosa and adjacent to the Pool of Bethesda is the remarkably preserved Crusader-era **Church of St. Anne** (near the Lion's Gate in the Old City off Sha'ar HaArayot St., 8am-noon and 2pm-5pm Mon.-Sat., NIS10). Catholic tradition says this is the birthplace of the Virgin Mary, which is preserved as a cave dwelling located beneath the crypt of the church.

The **Pool of Bethesda** (included with paid entry to the Church of St. Anne) is mentioned in the New Testament as the place where Jesus cured a crippled man. The area is an archaeological site that includes five pools and ruins of Byzantine, Crusader, and medieval churches.

ROCKEFELLER ARCHAEOLOGICAL MUSEUM

The **Rockefeller Archaeological Museum** (27 Sultan Suleiman St., tel. 02/670-8074, www.imj.org.il under Archaeology, 10am-3pm Sun.-Mon. and Wed.-Thurs., 10am-2pm Sat., free) is recommended by most locals and home to thousands of artifacts displayed in chronological order from prehistoric times to the Ottoman period. Among the treasures are a 9,000-year-old statue from Jericho, pieces of gold jewelry from the Bronze Age, and a collection of four dozen photographs of pioneering archaeologists in the region.

LADY TUNSHUQ PALACE

The 14th-century **Lady Tunshuq Palace** (off of Al Wad St. on Aqabat al-Taqiya, 24 hours, free) was built by Muslim Sufi mystics under the direction of Lady Tunshuq. The complex includes large archways with intricate inlaid marble work and also houses a working school.

TEMPLE MOUNT—AL HARAM AL-SHARIF

On the eastern side of the Old City is **Temple Mount—Al Haram al-Sharif** (main access for non-Muslims is between the Western Wall and Dung Gate, tel. 02/622-6250, www.noblesanctuary.com, 7:30am-11am and

the Dome of the Rock

Sun.-Thurs. Oct.-Mar., dress modestly, bring passport, entrance subject to change, free). The complex consists of about 100 buildings known as the Noble Sanctuary and an open plaza with ancient paving stones. The current construction dates back 1,400 years and includes the Dome of the Rock, Mount Moriah, Al Aqsa Mosque, and many other significant religious and cultural sites. It dates back much earlier, though, as it was the site of the first and second Jewish temples, and is one of the most hotly disputed pieces of territory in the world. Exercise caution doing anything resembling praying in the area because of tensions over religious and territorial claims. Guided tours are sometimes available at the information boxes on the plaza, but it is best to hire a guide in advance.

The **Dome of the Rock** is easily recognizable from many points in Jerusalem by its enormous golden dome. Situated atop Temple Mount on the edge of the Old City, the Dome of the Rock is built over the rock where, according to tradition, Prophet Muhammad ascended to heaven and Abraham attempted to sacrifice his son.

Al Aqsa Mosque is the third holiest site in Islam and a popular place for Muslims in Israel and the West Bank to pray, particularly for Friday prayers and major holidays.

The Islamic Museum of Temple Mount (southwest corner of the compound grounds, near the Western Wall, tel. 02/628-3313, 8am-11:30am and 2pm-4pm Mon.-Sat., NIS38 at stone kiosk between Al Aqsa Mosque and the Dome of the Rock) is one of the oldest museums in the country and houses a large collection of Korans, coins, glassware, guns, swords, daggers, and Islamic ceramics. The admission fee will also allow you to enter the mosque depending on the security situation at the time.

The Jewish Quarter
★ WESTERN WALL

Just down from Temple Mount is the most famed religious site in all of Judaism. Named for its position as the outer western wall of the destroyed Second Temple's courtyard, the **Western Wall** (Jewish Quarter of the Old City, tel. 02/627-1333, http://english.thekotel.org, www.jewish-quarter.org.il, 24 hours daily, free, extremely crowded on certain holidays, modest dress required) is also called the Wailing Wall or the Kotel.

The Wall is considered particularly significant to Jews because it is the last remaining piece of the great temple, the most significant site in all of Judaism. The imposing wall is the destination for the faithful who come to pray before it. Modest dress is required at all times. Space to pray is divided for men on the left and women on the right, and visitors are permitted to leave small pieces of paper with prayers or messages in the crevices of the wall. You can walk freely about the plaza and take photographs. An upper plaza in the southeastern corner offers an excellent view of the wall and the golden Dome of the Rock behind it.

On the northern end of the Kotel is the **Chain of Generations Center**

SIGHTS

(near the Western Wall, tel. 02/627-1333, http://english.thekotel.org, visits by reservation in advance Sun.-Thurs. and Fri. morning, NIS20, children NIS10), which tells the story of the Jewish people over 3,500 years and spans history from exile to statehood. The center uses a combination of music, sculpture, archaeology, and light effects and is divided into several rooms. Each room covers a different period and has works of art made from layers of glass lit up by rays of light that shine from dark rooms. There is also a view of the Western Wall from one of portion of the center.

Go south from the Western Wall toward Dung Gate and you will come upon the **Western Wall Excavations** (Western Wall, Jewish Quarter, tel. 02/627-1333, http://english.thekotel.org follow link to Tunnels, www.jewish-quarter.org.il, 7am-11pm Sun.-Thurs., depending on reservations, 7am-noon Fri. and holiday eves, adult NIS25, child NIS15). This 75-minute underground tour of excavations tells the story of ancient Jerusalem and explores hidden layers of the Western Wall. Tours are given only by reservation in advance and with a guide.

HERODIAN QUARTER AND WOHL ARCHAEOLOGICAL MUSEUM

A six-house compound on the slope of the hill facing the Temple Mount makes up the **Herodian Quarter and Wohl Archaeological Museum** (1 Ha-Karaim St., tel. 02/626-5922, www.jewish-quarter.org.il, 9am-5pm Sun.-Thurs., 9am-1pm Fri. and on eve of Jewish holidays, NIS18, combined ticket with the Burnt House NIS35). Here you'll find three main attractions: the Western House, the Middle Complex, and the Palatial Mansion. All thought to be homes of aristocrats and priests during the Herodian period, they are designed in the Hellenistic/Roman style. The 600-square-meter Palatial Mansion is the largest and gives clues to the lifestyle of the wealthy of that time. It includes rich floor mosaics and remarkably preserved wall

The Western Wall draws crowds at all times.

HURVA SYNAGOGUE

The distinctive large, white roof of Hurva Synagogue (89 Ha-Yehudim
St., tel. 02/626-5922, www.rova-yehudi.org.il, 9am-5pm Sun.-Thurs. and
9am-1pm Fri., NIS30) is home to the world's tallest Holy Ark and boasts
a 360-degree view of Jerusalem from the synagogue's roof rampart. The
synagogue, which literally means "ruin" in Hebrew, has a long and winding history. Construction began on it in 1700, but 20 years later it was still
not complete, and the unfinished building was torched and destroyed for
the first time. It was rebuilt in the mid-1800s, only to be blown up by the
Transjordan Legion Army just after the War of Independence in 1948.
When the Old City was recaptured by Israel in 1967, the site of the ruins was
commemorated but nothing was rebuilt there until 40 years later. In 2005,
construction on the current Hurva Synagogue began, and it was finished
in early 2010. The basement of the synagogue is home to antiquities, and
the masterfully renovated building integrates stones from the ruins of the
old building with the new. Entry for women is restricted at certain times,
but at prayer time it is less restrictive.

BURNT HOUSE MUSEUM

The Burnt House Museum (Tiferet Israel St., tel. 02/626-5921, www.rova-
yehudi.org.il, 9am-5pm Sun.-Thurs., 9am-1pm Fri. and on eve of Jewish
holidays, NIS30, combined ticket with Herodian Quarter NIS35) is the
excavated remains of the home of an upper-class priestly Jewish family
that burned during the destruction of the Second Temple in 70 BC. The
home was later excavated and features unique period archaeological artifacts and a multimedia presentation about the daily life of the people who
lived in the house. The movie is screened every 40 minutes starting at 9am.

RACHEL BEN ZVI CENTER

Across from the Israelite Tower is the Rachel Ben Zvi Center (7 Bonei ha-
Khoma, tel. 02/628-6288, www.ybz.org.il, 9am-4pm Sun.-Thurs., NIS10)
is a great place to stop off and see a scale model of the First Temple and
educational programming that includes an audiovisual history from 1000
to 586 BC.

RAMBAN SYNAGOGUE

The Ramban Synagogue (enter via Jewish Quarter St., tel. 02/627-1422,
call in advance to visit, modest dress required) is the second oldest working synagogue in the Old City. It is believed to have been built on Mount
Zion and then moved to the Old City in the 14th century. Closed by the
Ottomans in 1589, it was reopened in 1967. The synagogue is a small, modest building that many see as a symbol of the enduring power of faith, hope,
and tradition.

The **Cardo** (HaKardo St., tel. 02/626-5900, ext. 102, www.jewish-quarter.
org.il, 8am-6pm Sun.-Thurs., 8am-4pm Fri., closed for Shabbat, free) is the
impressive remnants of an ancient Roman double-columned main street
(always called a *cardo maximus*) and its shops that were a fixture in many
Roman cities. The Old City's Cardo stretched from the Damascus Gate to
the Zion Gate.

The southern section of the Cardo was excavated and buildings from
later periods were removed to reveal the Byzantine Cardo. Some of the columns from that period were reconstructed and restored, allowing visitors
to experience a taste of the 6th-century Cardo.

The covered section of the Cardo, which dates back to the Crusader
period, includes shops located in the same place as they were during ancient times. Most of the Cardo shops sell higher-end items like fine jewelry and Judaica.

Going north along the Cardo toward David Street you will come upon
the ruins of five Roman columns, where you'll find the original paving
stones of the street, dating to the Byzantine period. Farther on is a reproduction of a section of the Madaba Map, the oldest known map that depicts
Jerusalem in the 6th century.

The Armenian Quarter

This section of the Old City is largely residential and makes for a lovely and
distinctive place to take a quiet stroll.

ARMENIAN PATRIARCHATE OF ST. JAMES

Just inside Zion Gate and west until the city wall is the **Armenian
Patriarchate of St. James** (tel. 02/628-2331, www.armenian-patriarchate.
org, nourhan@netvision.net.il, 6:30am-7:30am and 3pm-3:30pm Mon.-Fri.,
8:30am-10:30am and 3pm-3:30pm Sat., free), or St. James Cathedral, with
its magnificent cathedral built on the tombs of St. James the Apostle and St.
James the brother of Jesus. The interior of the cathedral is decorated with
ancient hanging oil lamps and includes three chapels and two thrones at
the front of the church. The church served as a bomb shelter for residents
of the Armenian Quarter during the War of Independence in 1948.

CHRIST CHURCH

Near the intersection of Armenian Patriarchate Road and David Street is
Christ Church (Omar Ibn Al Hatab St. just inside Jaffa Gate, tel. 02/628-7487,
www.jerusalem-oldcity.org.il, www.cmj-israel.org, call in advance before visiting, NIS10), a compound on the right of the street. This is the oldest Protestant
church in the Middle East, and it houses a hostel, a heritage center, and a coffee shop. There is a tunnel beneath it dating to the Second Temple period.

A unique aspect of Christ Church is that it was completed in 1849 in preparation of the return of the Jews to Israel. The believers of the church wanted
to establish themselves in Jerusalem in order to be in a position to help the

Jews when they returned. Due to its history, there are Hebrew inscriptions
inside the church, and modern services have incorporated some Hebrew.

RAMPARTS WALK

For a unique view of Jerusalem, climb up onto the narrow catwalk on the
16th-century wall surrounding the Old City and try the **Ramparts Walk**
(Jaffa Gate, tel. 02/627-7550, 9am-4pm Sun.-Thurs., tickets for guided tours
at tourist service office, call in advance as tours vary widely by season,
self-guided ticket good for two days, NIS16). The southern route starts at
the Tower of David and ends at the Dung Gate, the northern route starts
at Jaffa Gate and ends at the Lion's Gate. You can also walk around the entire rampart in 3-4 hours or descend at any one of the gates along the way
after about 20 minutes. On the ramparts you will see a bird's-eye view of
the city, the ancient niches in the wall that used to be used by shooters to
defend the city, and many steep steps. There are modern, secure railings
along the way but it would be a tiring route for the very young or infirm.

TOWER OF DAVID MUSEUM

Just south of Jaffa Gate is the **Tower of David Museum** (tel. 02/626-5333,
www.towerofdavid.org.il, 10am-4pm Sun.-Thurs., 10am-2pm Sat. and holidays Sept.-June, 10am-5pm Sat.-Wed., 10am-7pm Thurs., 10am-2pm Fri.
July-Aug., adult NIS30, senior and child NIS15), located in a medieval citadel. The museum tells the story of Jerusalem and includes the archaeological site of the citadel. It is also home to a unique sound and light show,
the **Night Spectacular** (9pm and 10:30pm, adult NIS55, senior and child
NIS45; museum admission plus show adult NIS70, senior and child NIS55).

Mount Zion

Just outside of **Zion Gate** and a short walk up the hillside is **Mount Zion,**
which consists of a series of sites that can be visited in succession. Start

the Ramparts Walk around the Old City

with **Dormition Abbey** (Mount Zion, tel. 02/565-5330, www.dormitio. net, 8am-noon and 2pm-6pm daily, free), an active abbey with a distinctive bell tower and lead-covered cupola that can be seen from many points in the city. According to Christian tradition, Mount Zion is an important place in Jerusalem that was the meeting point for Jesus and his disciples.

You can enter Dormition Abbey, built near the place where Catholic tradition says the Virgin Mary ascended to heaven, and tour the German Benedictine basilica that was finished in 1910. Several mosaics can be seen inside the abbey, including some from a former Byzantine church that was previously at the same location.

Also on Mount Zion is **King David's Tomb** (Mount Zion compound, 8am-6pm and until 2pm on Fri., free) and **St. Mark's Church** (Ararat St., tel. 02/628-3304, 8am-6pm daily, free) or Monastery of St. Mark—the possible site of the Last Supper. King David's Tomb and the Room of the Last Supper can be visited with a short walk from the basement level (the tomb) to a nearby room of stone with enclaves and support pillars. Be wary if you are invited to make a donation to see either site, as there is no fee to enter. There is some dispute about the veracity of claims made about both the tomb and the supposed Room of the Last Supper due to centuries of war and subsequent destruction and rebuilding in the area. Docents will openly tell you that some theorize that the actual sites are a bit farther downhill.

CITY CENTER
Museum of Italian Jewish Art

Conveniently situated in the midst of City Center, the **Museum of Italian Jewish Art** (25 Hillel St., tel. 02/624-1610, http://ijamuseum.com, 10:30am-4:30pm Sun., Tues., Wed., noon-7pm Thurs., 10am-1pm Fri., NIS12) is a renowned as a repository of the history of Italian Jewry. Most famous among

Dormition Abbey on Mount Zion

its treasures of ritual Jewish objects from the baroque and Renaissance periods is a lavish gold 18th-century synagogue that was transported from Italy to Israel. The museum features permanent and changing exhibitions and is part of the Jerusalemite Star, five boutique museums that are physically connected and form the shape of the Star of David.

Museum of Tolerance

Slated to open at some point in 2017, the **Museum of Tolerance** (Gershon Agron St.) will be part museum and part commercial and residential housing units. The venture is being run under the behest of the Simon Wiesenthal Center and will feature a vast museum. The controversial project faced criticism during construction due to its location on the site of an old Muslim cemetery.

Jerusalem Time Elevator

The unique trip through Jerusalem's history offered by the **Jerusalem Time Elevator** (37 Hillel St., Agron House, tel. 02/624-8381, www.time-elevator-jerusalem.co.il, 10am-5pm Sun.-Thurs., 10am-2pm Fri., noon-6pm Sat., adult NIS54, senior NIS46, Internet booking NIS46, reservation recommended) is a sensory overload of 3,000 years of history in 2D surround sound, interactive environment. Using crashing ceilings, splashing water, and other special effects, the Time Elevator works well for groups or families whose energy has been spent with long walks in the hot sun from one archaeological site to another.

Ticho House (Israel Museum)

Built by an Arab dignitary in the latter half of the 19th century, the **Ticho House** (9 Harav Kook St., tel. 02/624-5068, www.go-out.com/ticho, 10am-5pm Sun.-Mon. and Wed.-Thurs., 10am-10pm Tues., 10am-2pm Fri., free) was one of the first houses constructed outside of the Old City walls and recently underwent a major renovation. It was home to well-known painter Anna Ticho in the early 20th century. Now part of the Israel Museum, today it has cozy art galleries, a collection of Hanukkah lamps, and a **reference library** (11am-6pm Sun.-Mon. and Thurs., 2pm-6pm Tues., 10am-noon Fri., free) of books about art, literature, and Jerusalem. It is an easy museum stop if you want a change of pace from busy Tolerance Square just outside.

Gush Katif Museum

The small but extremely unique **Gush Katif Museum** (5 Sha'arei Tsedek, tel. 02/625-5456, www.gushkatif.022.co.il, 10am-6pm Sun.-Thurs., 9am-1pm Fri., NIS20) is the only museum in the world that tells the story of the Jewish settlement Gush Katif in the Gaza Strip before it was broken apart in the 2005 unilateral disengagement when Israel pulled out of the region.

Jerusalem Great Synagogue

The unmistakable facade of the **Jerusalem Great Synagogue** (56 King

George St., tel. 02/623-0628, www.jerusalemgreatsynagogue.com, tours by appointment only by emailing jgs@zahav.net.il), an imposing structure that was opened in 1982 and dedicated to the memory of the six million Jewish victims of the Holocaust, can be seen easily as you drive by. The synagogue's internationally acclaimed choir is one of the world's chief repositories for Jewish Ashkenazic liturgical music, and massive stained glass windows adorn the main building. The synagogue's annual operating budget of US$1 million comes entirely from donations.

Hechal Shlomo Jewish Heritage Center

A landmark building in the city is the **Hechal Shlomo Jewish Heritage Center** (58 King George St., tel. 02/588-9010, http://eng.hechalshlomo.org.il, 9am-3pm Sun.-Thurs., adult NIS20, senior and child NIS15, family NIS50), which serves as a Jewish spiritual and cultural center. Aside from Hechal Shlomo's cultural events that include live music and its several permanent exhibits, it also houses the 300-year-old **Renanim Synagogue,** which was transported from Italy and features an Italian Ark. The active synagogue is decorated lavishly in 18th-century Italian style and is also home to the **Wolfson Museum of Jewish Art** with its permanent exhibit of Jewish ceremonial art and temporary exhibits of Israeli artists.

Museum on the Seam

On the old border between East and West Jerusalem is the **Museum on the Seam** (4 Chel Handasa St., tel. 02/628-1278, www.mots.org.il, 10am-5pm Sun.-Thurs., 10am-2pm Fri., adult NIS30, senior and student NIS25), a sociopolitical contemporary art museum that focuses on the social situation created by regional conflict. Established in 1999, the museum is not well known among locals, but comes highly recommended by visitors to Jerusalem who are interested in learning more about the regional conflict and artistic interpretations of their effect on the residents of the city.

EAST JERUSALEM
★ Mount of Olives

East from the Lion's Gate of the Old City is the **Mount of Olives** (www.mountofolives.co.il) which stretches from the **Kidron Valley** (24 hours daily, free) to the uppermost ridge at the end of E-Sheikh Street. Kidron Valley is where the tombs of Zechariah, Bnei-Hezir, and Absalom can be found, which are actually rather massive ancient structures and not simple gravestones. The tombs are the oldest graves of the ancient **Jewish Cemetery** (tel. 02/627-5050 for help locating a grave or to arrange a memorial service), which is considered by Jews to be sacred and the future sight of the resurrection. The oldest Jewish cemetery in the world, it covers the entire western and much of the southern slope of the Mount of Olives and is not technically open for public access, although there are no gates to keep people out.

Start or end your journey at the **Rehav'am Lookout** (turn off from

Jericho Rd. and go uphill until the road runs out, follow the signs, free parking), one of the highest points in Jerusalem. From April-September, try to get here before 10am or after 4pm to enjoy the unbelievable view without the heat.

Due to the sacredness of the Mount of Olives to Christianity, Judaism, and Islam, there are several holy sites in the area. If you start from the base of the Mount of Olives, go north along Al-Mansuriya Road and then west along El Monsuriyya toward the **Church of the Assumption** or the **Tomb of the Virgin Mary** (intersection of Jericho Rd. and Al-Mansuriya Rd., 6am-noon and 2:30pm-5pm Mon.-Sat., free), an underground tomb thought to be the resting place of the Virgin Mary. The site also includes a place for Muslims to pray, as St. Mary is highly regarded in Muslim tradition. Above the tomb is the 12th-century church. You can enter the tomb area via a set of wide steps that go underground.

Just south of Mary's Tomb on Jericho Road is the **Basilica of the Agony** or the **Church of All Nations** (Jericho Rd., tel. 02/628-4371, 8am-noon and 2pm-4:30pm Mon.-Sat., free), with a magnificent mosaic on the front and a row of pillars directly facing the road. The church was completed in 1924 with donations from a dozen different countries. The impressive interior of the church includes massive frescoes painted on vaulted walls and a large rock believed to be the place where Jesus prayed the night he was betrayed. The symbols of the 12 countries that contributed to the building of the church are woven into the 12 inlaid gold cupola ceilings.

Accessible from an alley toward the north side of the church is the **Garden of Gethsemane** (8am-noon and 2pm-6pm Mon.-Sat., free), where Jesus is said to have been betrayed by Judas. The garden is a grove of ancient olive trees, some of which are over 2,000 years old. It is completely

olive trees in the Garden of Gethsemane

surrounded by a wrought-iron fence, making it impossible to touch the trees or sit or walk among them.

Farther up the hill is the Franciscan **Dominus Flevit Church** (accessible by a footpath from the base of the Basilica of Agony or from the top of the Mount of Olives, tel. 02/627-4931, 8am-noon and 2pm-5pm Mon.-Sat., free), on a site considered holy as far back as the Bronze Age. The current structure was built in 1954 over the ruins of other buildings that have stood at the location, including a Byzantine period monastery and church whose mosaic floor can still be seen to the left of the entrance. The building, which is adjacent to the Mount of Olives cemetery, has a roof with a tear-shaped dome. This is the site where Jesus is said to have looked over Jerusalem and wept at its future destruction.

Farther up the road is the **Church of the Pater Noster** (E-Sheikh St., tel. 02/626-4904, 8:30am-noon and 2:30pm-4:30pm Mon.-Sat., NIS7), the traditional place where Jesus taught his disciples the Lord's Prayer. It is famed for the 140 inscriptions of the Lord's Prayer throughout the church in different languages.

Near the Garden of Gethsemane are the golden domes of the **Russian Orthodox Church of St. Mary Magdalene** (Al-Mansuriya Rd., tel. 02/628-4371, www.jerusalem-mission.org, 10am-11:30am Tues. and Thurs., free), impossible to miss with its Russian architecture built in the Muscovite style with golden onion domes or cupolas.

Finally, grouped near one another are the **Dome and Chapel of the Ascension** (al-Tur Village on Rub'a el-Adawiya St., tel. 02/628-4373, www.jerusalem-mission.org, 8am-6pm daily, NIS5), where Jesus is said to have risen to heaven 40 days after his resurrection, and the **Greek Orthodox Church of Viri Galilaei** (just north of the Chapel of the Ascension, left off Rub'a el-Adawiya St., free), a small Greek Orthodox church that is another of the three places on the Mount of Olives marking Jesus's ascension to heaven. The church is surrounded by an olive grove.

Jerusalem Archaeological Park

The **Jerusalem Archaeological Park** (Temple Mount Excavations, near the Old City's Dung Gate, tel. 02/627-7550, www.archpark.org.il, 8am-5pm Sun.-Thurs., 8am-2pm Fri., adult NIS30, senior, student, and child NIS16) covers a vast area near the Old City. The park extends from the north at Temple Mount to the slope of the Mount of

Jerusalem Archaeological Park

Olives and the Kidron Valley on the east, and on the west and south to the **45**
Valley of Hinnom.

Considered one of Israel's most significant antiquities site, it includes 5,000 years of history from the Canaanite (Bronze) Age and through the days of the Israelite monarchy in the First Temple period. At the entrance to the park is the **Davidson Center,** a virtual reconstruction and exhibition center that uses state-of-the-art computer technology to give visitors a historical and archaeological orientation.

★ CITY OF DAVID

The **City of David** (off Ophel St. in Silwan, tel. 02/626-8700, www.cityof-david.org.il, 8am-5pm Sun.-Thurs., 8am-2pm Fri. Nov.-Mar., 8am-7pm Sun.-Thurs., 8am-4pm Fri. Apr.-Oct., closed for Shabbat and holidays, adult NIS29, senior and child NIS15, 3D film add NIS13, guided tour adult NIS45 and senior and child NIS35) is controversial for its location in the Arab neighborhood of Silwan but fascinating for the many historical and archaeological treasures that it encompasses. Part of the controversy over the City of David is the claim that its very existence is a surreptitious attempt to circumvent the law and establish an Israeli presence in East Jerusalem. It is home to numerous important archaeological excavations and historical artifacts that bring the history of Jerusalem and the region to life.

Among the highlights in the City of David is the incredible **Hezekiah's Tunnel,** which is a wonder of ancient engineering. The tunnel starts at **Gihon Spring,** a major source of water for ancient Jerusalem for 1,000 years. If you are adventurous (and not claustrophobic) you can wade through the 2,700-year-old tunnel for 580 yards to the **Pool of Siloam,** the source for drawing water during biblical times. Make sure to bring a flashlight with you. The tunnel was built by King Hezekiah in preparation for the Syrian siege and was painstakingly chipped away by hand by two groups of workers. One group started from the top and the other from the bottom, and they met in the middle to join the tunnel and ensure the safety of the city's water supply from impending invaders.

the Pool of Siloam, where Hezekiah's Tunnel ends

Also in the City of David, the **Temple Mount Sifting Project** (entrance to Emek Tzurim National Park on the ascent to the Mt. of Olives, tel. 02/628-0342, templemount.wordpress.com, 8am-4pm Sun.-Thurs., 8am-1pm Fri. Nov.-Mar., 9am-5pm Sun.-Thurs., 8am-1pm Fri. Apr.-Oct., closed for Shabbat and holidays, adult NIS20, senior and child

The Separation Barrier

At several points near the Old City and at the border of East and West Jerusalem, you will be able to clearly see the Separation Barrier, also known as the Security Barrier, that separates Israel from the West Bank. The barrier directly abuts neighborhoods and villages along its route, and is not complete. If completed, it would span a distance of about 708 miles from north to south. It is currently about 440 miles long, and the structure varies from fence with barbed wire to concrete walls. Throughout Jerusalem it is mostly concrete.

NIS16, reservation required, free parking) affords a rare experience for the most curious of visitors. The project offers a two-hour participatory archaeological experience. You can sift through rubble that was dug up and dumped during construction and then reclaimed for the purpose of checking for ancient treasures. Any findings during the sifting tour are explained by archaeologists and expert guides at the site.

Garden Tomb

A slightly off-the-beaten-path location not far from the Old City is the **Garden Tomb** (Conrad Schick St., tel. 02/627-2745, www.gardentomb.com, 8:30am-noon and 2pm-5:30pm Mon.-Sat., free), the only place in Jerusalem other than the Church of the Holy Sepulchre that claims to be the site of the resurrection of Jesus. You can enter the cave in the hillside where it is said that Jesus was buried and inspect clues in the hillside that were said to correlate with historical references to his true burial place.

St. Stephen Basilica

Home to the world-famous Ecole Biblique (French Biblical and Archaeological School) is **St. Stephen Basilica** (6 Nablus Rd., tel. 02/626-4468, www.ebaf.edu, call in advance to visit as there is a locked gate, free). The original church at this location was built at the end of the 5th century as a resting place for the relics of St. Stephen, the first Christian martyr. The massive adjacent monastery was home to an unbelievable 10,000 monks by the end of the 6th century. Destroyed in the 12th century by Crusaders, it was not until 1900 that a new church was rededicated at the site on the base of the ruins. Founded in 1890, the Ecole is the oldest research institute in the Holy Land and has an extensive collection of 20,000 glass photo plates dating from 1890 that are partially on exhibit.

Tomb of the Kings

The **Tomb of the Kings** (entrance at the corner of Salah a-Din Street and Nablus Road, no formal visiting hours so ring bell, NIS3) is a popular tourist destination as one of the largest and most luxurious tombs in the area. A sign that says "Tombeau des Rois" is situated to left of stairs and a French flag flies above the sight. Enter through a metal gate that leads to a large courtyard dug out of stone to a depth of about 30 feet and the 2,000-year-old family tomb of Queen Helena of the Mesopotamian province of Adiabene. Two channels next to the stairs lead down to ritual baths, and there are about four dozen graves at the site, though grave robbers have long since made off with the contents. The area covers several acres and includes a tunnel that you can crawl through to reach the burial chamber, so bring a flashlight.

WEST JERUSALEM

German Colony

The Templar neighborhood of the **German Colony** (available tours vary, tel. 02/531-4600) is home to numerous historic buildings constructed in the mid-1800s by a group of German Protestants who came to the Holy Land in anticipation of the return of Jesus. There is also a German Colony in Haifa. The buildings in the area, one of Jerusalem's most affluent neighborhoods, are largely residential. It makes the perfect place to start or end a stroll to the nearby shopping and dining on Emek Refaim Street or HaTachana (First Station).

L.A. Mayer Museum for Islamic Art

Home to a small but exquisite collection of Islamic art and antique watches and clocks, the **L.A. Mayer Museum for Islamic Art** (2 HaPalmach St., tel. 02/566-1291, www.islamicart.co.il, 10am-3pm Sun.-Thurs., until 7pm Tues. and Thurs., 10am-2pm Fri. and eves of holidays, 10am-4pm Sat. and holidays, adult NIS40, student NIS30, child NIS20) also features rotating exhibitions.

★ The Israel Museum

The crown jewel of the unofficial museum district of Jerusalem is **The Israel Museum** (11 Ruppin St., near the intersection with Kaplan St., tel. 02/670-8811, www.imj.org.il, 10am-5pm Sat.-Mon. and Wed.-Thurs. and holidays, 4pm-9pm Tues., 10am-2pm Fri. and holiday eves, adult NIS54, student NIS39, senior, child, and disabled NIS27, NIS27 on repeat visit within 3 months only at box office, paid parking). Even among locals, the Israel Museum is lauded as one of the must-see spots in the city. Home to the Shrine of the Book and the Dead Sea Scrolls, the museum finished a major renovation in 2010 throughout its 20-acre campus to increase exhibition space, expand structures, and add exhibits.

The museum was founded in 1965 and is Israel's largest cultural institution. It also enjoys the renown of being one of the best art and archaeology museums in the world. It is home to artifacts from prehistory to the present time, and has the most extensive biblical and Holy Land archaeology collection in the world.

Among the museum's most spectacular collections are the Dead Sea Scrolls, housed in the unusual-looking building called the Shrine of the Book. You will also want to see the outdoor model of the Second Temple, which covers almost one acre. There is enough here for several hours with a meal at the restaurant along the way, where you can rub shoulders with famous locals.

Jerusalem Biblical Zoo

The **Jerusalem Biblical Zoo** (1 Aharon Sholov Rd., tel. 02/675-0111, www.jerusalemzoo.org.il, 9am-5pm Sun.-Thurs., 9am-4:30pm Fri. and holiday eves, 10am-5pm Sat. and holidays, adult NIS55, child, senior, and student NIS42) is a remarkably diverse zoo that is also a nonprofit organization owned equally by the Municipality of Jerusalem, the Jerusalem Foundation, and the Jerusalem Development Authority. Opened in 1993, it is home to an incredibly wide array of animals, including monkeys, elephants, lions, lemurs, snakes, flamingos, and more.

National Campus for the Archaeology of Israel

Expected to open sometime in 2017, the **National Campus for the Archaeology of Israel** (Hamuze'onim St., www.archaeology.org.il) will and act as a center for research, study, education, and exhibition of the vast collection of Israeli Antiquities Authority materials excavated in Israel. The approximately two million objects in the Archaeological State Treasures will be housed under one roof on the campus for academic and public access.

Bible Lands Museum

The first museum in the world dedicated to the history of the Bible and the ancient Near East is the **Bible Lands Museum** (25 Avraham Granot St., tel. 02/561-1066, www.blmj.org, 9:30am-5:30pm Sun.-Thurs., closes at 9:30pm

a model of the Second Temple at the Israel Museum

NIS22). The permanent exhibition, which is made up almost entirely of the former private collection of Dr. Elie Borowski, art collector and academic, spans from earliest civilization to the early Christian era in the lands of the Bible. The classical art collection features Etruscan, Greek, and Roman art from the 7th century BC through the 2nd century AD. A collection of well-preserved frescoes is believed to be from a village near Pompeii.

Bloomfield Museum of Science

The small but ambitious **Bloomfield Museum of Science** (Hebrew University on Museum Blvd., tel. 02/654-4888, www.mada.org.il, 10am-6pm Mon.-Thurs. and until 8pm in Aug., 10am-2pm Fri., 10am-3pm Sat., NIS45, senior NIS20, children under 5 free) is a very hands-on, interactive museum designed for very young children to about age 12. Consisting of three above-ground levels and two below-ground levels and indoor and outdoor exhibits, the museum is full of science lessons that are built to be played and experimented with. Some of them are a bit worn from excessive play, but it's easy to move on. The museum also hosts rotating exhibits, special events, and has an underground auditorium for shows. A small cafeteria is inside.

National Government Compound

A grouping of significant government buildings, some of which are open for tourists to visit, is known as the **National Government Compound.**

A visit to **The Knesset (Parliament)** (intersection of Kaplan St. and Rothschild St. in Givat Ram, tel. 02/675-3337, www.knesset.gov.il, tours@knesset.gov.il, tours 8:30am-2pm Sun.-Thurs., English tours 8:30am, noon, and 2pm Sun.-Thurs., reservations not needed for individuals, just show up 30 minutes before tour starts, free) should include a guided tour, as you will be unable to enter the building unaccompanied. The very general tour touches on the workings of the Knesset, artwork in the Knesset, architecture, and a combined tour with the Supreme Court. The only independent tour is the Knesset Archaeology Park tour, which includes findings from the Second Temple period through the Ottoman period.

Known for its grand architectural design created by the brother-sister team of Ram Karmi and Ada Karmi Melamede from Tel Aviv is the **Supreme Court of Israel** (intersection of Yitzhak Rabin St. and Rothschild St. in Givat Ram, tel. 02/675-9612, www.court.gov.il, English tours noon Sun.-Thurs., free). Opened in 1992, the building includes a massive restored mosaic, a panoramic window, and the unique library that is an architectural representation of the Second Temple. The overall structure was created to integrate postmodern architectural elements and reflect Jerusalem's rich architectural history. It was also designed to express the values of justice, law, and righteousness.

Monastery of the Cross

Resembling a fort, the Greek Orthodox **Monastery of the Cross** (enter on Shota Rustaveli St. in Rehavya Valley, tel. 02/679-0961, 10am-4:30pm Mon.-Sat., NIS10) was most recently rebuilt in the 11th century. The monastery is on the site where Christian tradition says the tree grew that was used to make the cross to crucify Jesus.

It was originally built in the 6th century, destroyed in the Persian invasion in 614, and rebuilt again in 1038. An important Christian theological seminary through the 20th century, it has 16th- and 17th-century frescoes and mosaics and includes a courtyard café.

★ Yad Vashem

Nothing can prepare you for the enormous psychological and emotional impact of visiting Yad Vashem. More of an institution than a museum, the **Yad Vashem** complex (enter via the Holland Junction, on the Herzl Route opposite the entrance to Mount Herzl and the descent to Ein Kerem, tel. 02/644-3802, www.yadvashem.org, 9am-5pm Sun.-Wed., 9am-8pm Thurs., 9am-2pm Fri. and holiday eves, closed Sat. and all Jewish holidays, free, no children under 10 years old in Holocaust History Museum and main exhibits, last visitor one hour before closing, paid parking, free shuttle from Mount Herzl stop on the light-rail) is an astounding window on Jewish history and culture. Because of the size of Yad Vashem and the amount of information, it is advisable to plan to spend at least half a day there.

Start with the **Holocaust History Museum**, the building behind the main entrance. You can rent an audio guide (NIS20) and buy a guide map (NIS10) and work your way through the 4,200-square-meter spike-shaped linear structure that stretches mostly underground. The museum includes

the entrance to Yad Vashem

an overwhelming collection, some of it interactive, of artifacts, firsthand testimonies, and personal possessions from the Holocaust.

As you work your way through the main museum, it ends in a skylight at the uppermost edge and the **Hall of Names**, a circular repository for the names and testimonies of the millions of Holocaust victims. Two million testimonies are included, with room for four million more. The somber and impressive **Hall of Remembrance** features basalt boulders from the Sea of Galilee and the always burning Eternal Flame surrounded by a mosaic of 22 names of the most notorious sites where Nazis committed murder. In front of the flame is a stone crypt with the ashes of Holocaust victims.

Home to the largest and most wide-ranging collection of Holocaust art in the entire world, the **Holocaust Art Museum** has some of its more than 10,000 pieces of work on display first by artist and then by subject matter. There are plenty of comfortable benches for lingering reflection, and the first computerized archive of Holocaust art and artists is adjacent to the museum's galleries.

Mount Herzl

At the entrance to the Yad Vashem campus, is **Mount Herzl** (Herzl Blvd., Mt. Herzl, tel. 02/632-1515, www.herzl.org, 8:30am-6pm Sun.-Wed. last tour at 5pm, 8:45am-8pm Thurs., 8:30am-1pm Fri. with last tour at 12:15pm, tours must be arranged in advance or on a first-come, first-served basis, NIS25, child NIS20). The museum here, dedicated to the story of famed Zionist Theodor Herzl, gives visitors an audiovisual history through a live action one-hour program. The four rooms of the small museum explore Herzl's path from a European to the modern father of the State of Israel and include artifacts and memorabilia. Mount Herzl is an easy stop on the way to Yad Vashem.

SPECIAL TOURS

Tour Guides

As with any major tourist destination, there are a number of fly-by-night tour guides and companies in Jerusalem selling their services. A good rule of thumb is to work with someone who is a licensed tour guide or get recommendations from the front desk at your hotel.

The **official travel website of Israel** (www.goisrael.com) has a complete listing of tour guides authorized by the Ministry of Tourism who offer services in a wide range of languages. You can also choose a guide who has a car as part of their services. Check under the "Before You Go" tab on the website, and choose "Tour Guide Search" from the left tab.

Asher Altshul (tel. 052/232-3219, www.asheraltshul.com) is a private licensed tour guide based in Jerusalem who is fluent in English and Hebrew.

Sandeman's New Europe (www.newjerusalemtours.com) is a large, international company with a good reputation that offers a variety of tours in Jerusalem, including free daily tours of the Old City. They can be contacted online in advance of any special tour you'd like to arrange.

Free Saturday Tours

Saturday is one of the best days of the week to go on a free tour in Jerusalem. Most of the city shuts down and doesn't start opening again until late Saturday evening so there is very little foot and vehicular traffic. It's also a good chance to explore some of Jerusalem's neighborhoods (for detailed tour listings by type, go to the **city's official tourism website** at www.itraveljerusalem.com).

Several types of three-hour-long Saturday tours depart at 10am from **Safra Square** (24-26 Yafo St., tel. 02/531-4600, call in advance, free).

- **The Explore Ethiopia Tour** explores Eliezer Ben Yehuda's old neighborhood (he was instrumental in reviving the Hebrew language) and also goes through the Russian Compound, The Ticho House, Ethiopia Street, Bnei Brit Library, and Beit Tavor Street.

- **The German Colony Tour** takes you through the neighborhood built by German Templars at the end of the 19th century and includes a route from King David Street down through Emek Refaim Valley.

- **The Hanevi'im Tour** takes visitors through the history of Hanevi'im Street and its ties to the British, Germans, Italians, and Ethiopians. Some of the buildings on the tour help tell the stories of famous leaders, ambassadors, doctors, poets, artists, and hermits.

- **The Kidron Valley Tour** explores the burial grounds of the Second Temple period, the Kidron River and its streams, and the story behind four rock-hewn graves here. The route goes through Jaffa Gate, the Jewish Quarter, Dung Gate, Kidron Valley viewpoint, and Kidron Valley proper.

- **The Muslim Quarter Tour** takes you from Damascus Gate in the Old City to the Western Wall.

- **The Rehavya Walking Tour** includes national institutions in the Rehavya neighborhood, including a monastery and the president of Israel's home.

- **Sandeman's New Jerusalem Tour** meets just inside the Old City's Jaffa Gate by the tourism information stand (11am and 2pm daily) and covers a broad range of sights during this two-hour tour. Look for the guides in the red Sandeman's T-shirts; guides might encourage you to tip them.

Nature Tours

The **Society for the Protection of Nature in Israel** (tel. 02/625-2357 or 03/638-8688, www.teva.org.il) gives urban walking tours in English, but not on a fixed schedule. You must call to see if an English tour is available, as they typically only take groups of 10 or more. Their website has a green map that contains useful information about green spaces within the city. They also give ecotours throughout Israel, including relatively cheap places to stay called field schools in remoter regions of the country. They can also be contacted in their U.S., Canadian, French, and British offices.

Archaeological Tours

For tours with an archaeological twist, try **Archaeological Seminars Institute Ltd.** (tel. 02/586-2011, www.archesem.com, US$200 and up, plus VAT and entrance fees) for one of their varied half- and full-day private walking tours for up to 10 people. Some of the tour types include archaeology as it relates to religion, and retracing the footsteps of ancient Jewish residents of the city.

Bus Tours

For those who would rather ride, Egged bus line's **Double-Decker Bus Tour** (tel. 03/920-3992, www.eggedtours.com, from 9am Sun.-Thurs., NIS200-400) can be a great way to see the city if you're independent

Underground Archaeological Tours

Above the ground, Jerusalem is rich and fascinating. Underground lies another layer of the city that will convince even the most frugal traveler of the value of paying for a tour. These are some of the best underground tours in Jerusalem:

Warren's Shaft

- **Burnt House:** Part of a larger complex under the Old City's Jewish Quarter, the remarkable charred remains date back to AD 70 (www.jewish-quarter.org.il).

- **Herodian Quarter and Wohl Archaeological Museum:** The basement of a Jewish seminary covers the remains of a mansion from the Second Temple period (www.jewish-quarter.org.il).

- **Hezekiah's Tunnel:** You can wade through the water in this 2,700-year-old tunnel, part of the City of David, for 580 yards (www.cityofdavid.org.il).

- **Warren's Shaft:** An underground waterworks system that dates back to the age of the kings of Judea was discovered in 1867 by British engineer Sir Charles Warren (www.cityofdavid.org.il).

- **The Western Wall Tunnels:** This 75-minute tour explores hidden layers of the Western Wall (http://english.thekotel.org).

enough to hop on and off the big red bus at some of the 24 stops that it makes. One- and two-day passes are available, and stops include several major tourist spots in Jerusalem, including Yad Vashem, the Botanical Garden, multiple locations around the Old City, the National Government Compound, and the Israel Museum. It also includes local shopping spots, like Malha Mall. Each seat is equipped with headphone guides in several languages. If you are organized enough and like to stay on a schedule, this could be an efficient way to hit several major sites with less transportation hassle and cost.

Entertainment and Events

Jerusalem, with its emphasis on ancient tradition and spiritual and family life, isn't typically known for its nightlife scene. But new initiatives by the city municipality and new ventures by industrious business owners have been slowly changing that in recent years. If you are looking for evening entertainment, you can find a select variety of bars, pubs, and live music clubs as well as performing arts venues. If you are looking for a club, be prepared to ask around to a lot of locals.

LIVE MUSIC BARS AND CLUBS
City Center

Not quite as lively at night as it is during the day, Machane Yehuda (the *shuk*) has varied entertainment tucked into its nooks and crannies. After the market closes for shopping, it keeps going for dining, drinks, and music. Start with **Casino de Paris** (Machane Yehuda 3, Machane Yehuda Market, tel. 02/650-4235, noon-2am, Sun.-Thurs., closed for Shabbat and opens again after 9pm on Sat., no cover), which was once the gathering place for British officers during the British Mandate period. Now revived to cater to the bar scene, it features a unique menu of cocktails and a limited fish and vegetable menu.

A restaurant-bar with a nightly offering of jazz music by local musicians, **Birman Musical Bistro** (8 Dorot Rishonim St., tel. 02/623-6115, 2pm-3am Sun.-Thurs., no cover) has a cozy atmosphere that includes a loft and couches. The menu features a selection of nonkosher Middle Eastern meat dishes.

Blaze Sport 'N' Rock Bar (23 Hillel St., tel. 054/816-5488, http://blazebar.co.il, 4pm-2am daily, no cover), just south of Ben Yehuda Street, is considered to be the closest thing to a biker bar in the city and owned by one of Jerusalem's leading thrash-metal musicians, Shworchtse Chaye's lead vocalist. Every night of the week the bar features live rock music and alternative bands, and the menu includes over 30 draught and bottled beers. They have live big-screen sports broadcasts.

The trendy **HaTaklit** (7 Heleni HaMalka St., tel. 02/624-4073, 8pm-last customer, no cover) was founded by three music industry Jerusalemites who adorned the walls with vinyl record sleeves. The full bar serves cocktails, and there is beer on tap, English football screenings, live music, DJs, and independent performers. The happy hour (4:30pm-9pm daily) includes buy one tap beer, get one free.

The **Bass Club** (1 Hahistadrut St., tel. 050/477-7791, http://bassclub. wordpress.com, daily 8pm until last customer, cover varies from about NIS30, call in advance) is known for its variety of music, featuring bass music as well as reggae and dancehall music nights.

Oliver Twist (59 Haneviim St., tel. 054/521-2044, 10pm-4:30am Thurs.-Sat., no cover) is a popular DJ club housed in a 150-year-old building that also serves food and has outdoor seating.

West Jerusalem

The bustling, warehouse-size club **17** (17 Haoman St., tel. 02/678-1658, 9pm-3am Tues., 9:30pm-5am Thurs., 9:30pm-3am Sat., NIS80) is known by its former name to locals (Haoman 17) and features Israeli music on Tuesdays, house music on Thursdays, and funk music on Saturdays. They regularly host international DJs.

The **Yellow Submarine** (13 Herkevim St., tel. 02/679-4040, http://yellowsubmarine.org.il, shows daily from around 8pm or later, entrance NIS30 and up depending on show) is a multidisciplinary music center and has a varied offering of live musical performances. It also houses rehearsal rooms, recording studios, and hosts an annual international music showcase.

The stylish and upscale **Zappa** (28 Derech Hevron, tel. 03/762-6666, www.zappa-club.co.il, price varies by show but generally NIS50 and up) features high-quality local and international music, light food and drinks, and a sizable stage for performers situated within a close distance to the audience, as well as some major names in jazz, rock, and reggae.

BARS, PUBS, AND WINE BARS
City Center

The Mamilla Hotel has a few nice spots for drinks and mingling. **Winery** (11 King Solomon St., 2nd Fl., tel. 02/548-2222, 3pm-8pm Sun.-Thurs., 2pm-6pm Fri., NIS40) has a selection of 300 Israeli wines that gives a nice introduction to the region's vines, and it sells kosher wines. The **Rooftop** (11 King Solomon St., 8th Fl., tel. 02/548-2222, 6pm-midnight Sun.-Thurs., noon-11pm Fri.-Sat. with a cold Shabbat menu, NIS85) offers a commanding view of Jerusalem and the Old City and caters to the wealthy and elite set. A long bar is complemented by a wooden deck and a row of small bar tables and stools near the front, while the back area (with the better view) has a larger area with seating for dinner. The posh **Mirror Bar** (11 King Solomon St., 2nd Fl., tel. 02/548-2230, www.mamillahotel.com, 8pm-last customer Sun.-Thurs., 9pm-last customer Sat., no cover) features a stylish, modern interior and a selection of cigars that can be enjoyed in a glassed-in smoking room.

Part of an Israeli chain but still a great time, **Dublin Irish Pub** (4 Shamai St., tel. 053/944-3740, http://dub.rest-e.co.il, 5pm-3am Sat.-Thurs., 5pm-5am Fri., no cover) features Gothic and Irish design elements with heavy wooden furniture from Ireland and serves 300 drinks and 70 different beers (18 on tap). The popular hangout has several flat-screen sports TVs, a happy hour (5pm-8pm daily), and a menu of nonkosher food.

Easily accessible from central Jaffa Road, **Heder Vehetsi** (31 Yafo St., tel. 054/642-4242, 6pm until late daily, no cover) is a popular hangout for university students and other 20-something patrons. They are known as one of few bars in town open on Friday night and for their inexpensive selection of alcohol.

The distinctly North American flavor of the crowd at **Mike's Place** (33 Yafo St., tel. 02/502-3439, www.mikesplacebars.com, 11am-last customer Sun.-Thurs. and until 3pm on Fri. and opens after 8pm on Sat., no cover) is part of the draw. This sports bar features booths and wood paneling, big-screen TVs, a kosher food menu, a global selection of beers, and a daily happy hour.

Inspired by traditional English pubs and decorated with a rich, cozy atmosphere of wood, **Bellwood Bar** (Yosef Rivlin and Hasorag St. 5, tel. 050/486-3333, www.bellwood.co.il, 5pm-midnight daily, no cover) features over 100 varieties of whiskey and 15 international beers on tap, as well as a robust food menu of classic pub items like fish-and-chips and hamburgers.

PERFORMING ARTS
Cultural Centers

If you're in the mood for something with an ethnic cultural flavor, **Beit Avi Chai** (44 King George St., tel. 02/621-5300, www.bac.org.il, 1pm-9:30pm Sun.-Thurs., 9:30am-noon Fri.) features speakers and artists, including Israeli musicians every Monday, a summer music concert series of Israeli musicians in the courtyard, and evening concerts by Jerusalem and Israeli musical favorites.

The **Gerard Behar Center** (11 Bezalel St., tel. 02/545-6868, http://gerard-behar.jerusalem.muni.il) is home to two acclaimed dance troupes, Kolben Dance Co. and Vertigo, and also plays host to independent productions and collaborations including their hot jazz series.

Extremely well done performances in English are hosted by the World Union for Progressive Judaism at **Beit Shmuel** (6 Eliyahu Shama St., tel. 02/620-3455, www.beitshmuel.com). They play host to a wide variety of staged performances including plays, musicals, ethnic music, and educational and cultural activities.

One of Jerusalem's finest centers for cultural activities is **Mishkenot Sha'ananim** (9 Yemin Moshe St., tel. 02/629-2220, www.mishkenot.org.il), which hosts a wide variety of festivals, screenings, and lectures, and is home to the INFO Press Club for foreign journalists.

The hot spot for families and those in the mood for some indoor/outdoor dining, shopping, and live music is the **First Station,** in Hebrew **HaTachana** (4 David Remez St., tel. 02/653-5239, http://firststation.co.il, open daily), centered around an outdoor stage under a tent where bands perform year-round for no charge. Free entry to the children's Gymboree tent on Thursdays also includes evening performances.

Theaters and Cinemas

The **Jerusalem International Convention Center** (1 Shazar Blvd., tel. 02/655-8558, www.iccjer.co.il) has the largest auditorium in Israel with 3,000 seats and is the home of the Israel Philharmonic Orchestra when they are in Jerusalem. It is part of a larger complex called Binyanei Ha'uma that also houses the **Globus Movie Theater** (tel. 02/622-3685).

The **Jerusalem Centre for the Performing Arts** (20 David Marcus, tel. 02/560-5757, www.jerusalem-theatre.co.il), with its five halls, hosts everything from musical performances to dance, festivals, plays, and films, and is home to the Jerusalem Symphony Orchestra. It is the largest center for performing arts and cultural performances in Israel.

For stage performances of plays and musicals, **The Khan Theatre** (2 David Remez Sq., tel. 02/630-3600 www.khan.co.il) offers a variety of performances in a quaint and intimate setting, including special children's performances by its company of permanent actors.

The **Jerusalem Cinematheque** (11 Derech Hevron, tel. 02/565-4356, www.jer-cin.org.il, NIS38) is an upper-crust movie theater that shows films both old and new from Europe and North America, as well as some television episodes, independent films, and live in HD performances. There is a concessions area, but no food is allowed in the theaters. Many moviegoers tend to eat at the Cinematheque's adjacent Lavan restaurant before or after a film.

The **Globus Movie Theater** (1 Shazar Blvd., tel. 02/622-3685) and **Rav**

There's fun for the whole family at the First Station.

ENTERTAINMENT AND EVENTS

Hen (19 Haoman, tel. 02/679-2799) both offer more standard-style theaters with multiplex settings and more mainstream American movies.

New addition **Cinema City** (10 Yitzhak Rabin Blvd., tel. 074/752-6700, www.cinemacity.co.il) is a massive complex that includes shopping, dining, and specialized theaters that are designed for children. It also features live stage performances, live high-definition broadcasting, and 3D movies.

FESTIVALS AND EVENTS

In the past few years, the number and types of festivals and music events taking place in the city have increased dramatically.

Ongoing

The Tower of David Museum hosts a **Night Spectacular** (south of the Old City's Jaffa Gate, tel. 02/626-5333, www.towerofdavid.org.il, 9pm and 10:30pm, adult NIS55, senior and child NIS45, or museum admission plus show adult NIS70, senior and child NIS55), where the outer walls of the Old City are used for an historic program using lights and images, accompanied by music.

Spring

The annual **International Writer's Festival** (writersfestival.co.il) is relatively new to Jerusalem, but its scope and scale are huge. The festival is held in late spring at Mishkenot Sha'ananim and features a week's worth of events, including talks with famous authors, film screenings, and events for kids. Many of the events are in English.

Summer

The **Jerusalem International Film Festival** (Jerusalem Cinematheque, www.jff.org.il) has been running for almost 30 years and is primarily focused on Israeli film.

Just as much fun as it sounds, the **Jerusalem Beer Festival** (Independence Park, tel. 050/594-8844, www.jerusalembeer.com/en) has been in action for over a decade and is staged in a central park on the grounds of the Old Train Station. Featuring about 30 different types of beers, both international and local, the festival lasts two days and includes live music.

The Old City comes alive every summer with **Balabasta** (www.gojerusalem.com, July) when the ancient streets are filled with live performances, art installations, eating contests, puppets, and DJs.

The **Jerusalem Woodstock Revival** (Kraft Stadium, tel. 03/613-3556, www.woodstockrevival.com, NIS85-140) features musical acts performing covers from Pink Floyd, Neil Young, Bob Dylan, and others who were at Woodstock.

The **Zion Reggae Festival** (Gan Sacher, tel. 03/602-3619) features major reggae performers including Ziggy Marley, Alpha Blondy, and Barrington Levy.

A bit more refined crowd can be found at the **Jerusalem Wine Festival** (Billy Rose Garden of the Israel Museum, tel. 02/625-9703, 8:30pm-11pm, NIS80/evening pp, includes a wineglass, unlimited tasting, and admission to the museum galleries until 9pm on Tues.), which takes place over three days at the end of July. The festival brings together some of the best wines from Israel's varied collection of local wineries.

The **End of the Summer Festival** (20 David Marcus, tel. 02/560-5755, www.jerusalem-theatre.co.il) is three days at the end of August of Israeli and foreign artists and performers. The festival consists of some of the latest work in performance art and film. It's hugely popular amongst locals.

Highly energetic and fascinating, **Contact Point** (Israel Museum, www.jerusalemseason.com/en, August) connects artists and audiences through a night of interactions that start at dusk and end at 3am. All contained within the campus of the Israel Museum, Contact Point features interactive art experiences, live music, dance, and access to the museum's permanent exhibitions.

Fall

The **Jerusalem International Chamber Music Festival** (YMCA Mary Nathaniel Hall, tel. 02/625-0444, www.jcmf.org.il, Sept., NIS80-150) is a several days-long concert series that highlights a different area of classical music every year.

For an interesting peek at Israeli culture, head to the **President's Open House** (Presidential residence, Hanasi St. in Talbiyeh, Sukkot week) for the traditional Sukkah, photo taking, and live music.

A series of other events take place during Sukkot week, check with the official tourism site of the **Jerusalem Municipality** (www.itraveljerusalem.com) for details and listings of events.

The **Abu Ghosh Vocal Music Festival** (www.agfestival.co.il/en) takes place every year in the Arab village of Abu Ghosh just outside of Jerusalem. Concerts are performed in the 12th-century Crusader-Benedictine Church in the heart of the village, and at the Kiryat Ye'arim Church.

Winter

Taking place for three decades, **The Jerusalem International Book Fair** (Central locations throughout Jerusalem, www.jbookfair.com, free) brings together agents, authors, and exhibitors of all kinds. The festival's Jerusalem Prize is awarded to a writer who exhibits the principles of individual freedom in society.

Shopping

Jerusalem has a wide variety of shops, with an emphasis on religious ornaments and objects, clothing, and locally handmade ceramics. Types of shopping can be divided mainly into Judaica, antiques, jewelry, gifts and souvenirs, regionally designed and manufactured clothing, and outdoor markets. Home decor and houseware shops, shopping malls, and furniture stores are largely concentrated in the neighborhood of Talpiyot. When buying anything of value, do not leave the shop without the proper paperwork for customs, and also make sure to ask for the **tax rebate** calculation on your receipt.

THE OLD CITY
Jaffa Gate

If you enter through Jaffa Gate, follow the flow of foot traffic as it goes past the **Ministry of Tourism Information Center** (1 Jaffa St., tel. 02/627-1422, 8:30am-5pm Sun.-Thurs., 8:30am-noon Fri.) to HaNotsrim Street, a narrow pedestrian street in the Christian Quarter where you can find **religious items, souvenirs, clothing, and jewelry** that should satisfy any urge you have for doing minor shopping and bargaining. If you stay on the main road from Jaffa Gate (David St.) until you reach the second to last right turn, you'll get to **HaKardo** or the **Cardo** (tel. 02/626-5900, ext. 102, business area and shops 8am-6pm Sun.-Thurs., 8am-4pm Fri.) with its numerous high-end gift shops and galleries for Judaica. This is the border between the Jewish and Armenian Quarters, the latter of which has some interesting shops that sell jewelry, antiques, and textiles.

Damascus Gate

For a vibrant shopping experience (as in, loud and extremely physical), just inside of Damascus Gate at the intersection of Beit Habad Street and

the entrance to the Old City's Jaffa Gate

Mamilla's Numbered Stones

Throughout Jerusalem you will see stone buildings with the curious characteristic of sequential numbers scrolled by hand on each stone. These are historically significant buildings that have been disassembled, preserved, and reassembled. The numbers have been left to indicate the act of preservation and to distinguish the building among its neighbors as having special historic value. It is also a way to honor the authenticity of Jerusalem as an ancient city.

Stroll through Mamilla Alrov Quarter, and you will see five such examples of buildings preserved in this way, either in their entirety or by being incorporated into new buildings. The preservation was done under the guidance of the Israel Antiquities Authority.

Two buildings in Mamilla that have been left in place are particularly notable. The Stern House, situated at about the center of Mamilla's pedestrian promenade, was built in 1877 and hosted Zionist Theodor Herzl on his only trip to Israel. The Clark House was constructed by American evangelicals in the late 19th century.

SHOPPING

El Wad Hagai Street is the gateway to the **Arab Souk,** where you can find trinkets, clothes, spices, sweets, jewelry, raw meat, and other food. Watch out for people running through with carts!

Mamilla

Though not technically connected, the Old City and Mamilla feed off of each other like a mountain and a river. Go down the stairs from the Old City's Jaffa Gate plaza and you'll reach the mellow atmosphere of **Mamilla** (street entrance is at the intersection of Shlomtsiyon HaMalka and Shlomo HaMelech, just across the street from the David Citadel Hotel, shop hours are generally 9am-10pm Sun.-Thurs., 9am-3pm Fri.). Many shops here are Israeli or international chain stores for clothing, jewelry, and makeup, which makes it a convenient place. There is also a chain pharmacy for SuperPharm. Brands represented include Rolex, MAC, H. Stern, Nike, Polo Ralph Lauren, Gap, Nautica, bebe, and Tommy Hilfiger, as well as local brands like Fox, Castro, Ronen Chen, and Steimatzky Books. You can also come across musical street performers here, which makes it a fun place to wander and window-shop, and it stays active late into the evening.

Take a look inside **Eden Fine Art** (Alrov Mamilla Ave., tel. 02/624-2506, www.eden-gallery.com) for a glimpse at this international art representative. The shop sponsors artwork, sculptures, and photographs from select leading Israeli and international artists. The bright, small venue caters to upper-crust clients and art collectors, and has some interesting pieces from Israeli artists.

The **Stern House** is a charming and interesting preserved and reconstructed building that played host to Theodor Herzl during his visit to Jerusalem in 1898, and now houses one of the **Steimatzky Books** chain store (tel. 02/625-7268), which has a good selection of English books and magazines, and a **Café Café** (tel. 02/624-4773) chain coffee shop, a place to get a bite to eat or coffee.

One of the leading jewelry chains in Israel, **Miller Jewelry** (tel. 02/622-3414) has a store on the smaller end in Mamilla with a highly selective number of their finest pieces.

CITY CENTER
Yafo Street (Jaffa Street)

Busy **Yafo Street** (also known as Jaffa Street) is the main artery of the city's center and home to the light-rail train. Only pedestrian and train traffic are allowed to go through the length of the street that runs through the heart of town, passing always-happening **Tolerance Square** (formerly known as **Zion Square**) near where Yafo intersects with Shamai Street, which is full of tourists, souvenir shops, ice cream shops, juice bars, and several sidewalk cafés.

Ben Yehuda Street (Pedestrian Mall)

A main pedestrian artery that leads to Tolerance Square, **Ben Yehuda Street** is full of shops that tend to cater to tourists and sell items such as souvenirs and Judaica. In the past, the highly trafficked area made it a target for terrorist bombings—look for silver plaques on the ground and sides of buildings marking spots where bombings took place. The triangle formed by Ben Yehuda, King George, and Yafo Streets is partially inhabited by shops founded after attacks on the Mamilla commercial center just days after the UN vote on the partition of Palestine in 1947.

★ Machane Yehuda Market (The *Shuk*)

Also accessible by Yafo Street is the open-air market world-famous for its

Shopping options abound in City Center.

colorful produce stands, restaurants, and characters, and known to locals as the *shuk*. **Machane Yehuda Market** (between Yafo St. and Agripas St. at Beit Ya'acov and Eitz HaChaim, www.machne.co.il/en, 8am-7pm Sun.-Thurs., 8am-3pm Fri.) is overwhelming in its sights, sounds, and tastes. No matter which entrance you take (and there are about a half a dozen ways to go in), you will find yourself in a seemingly endless maze of bins overflowing with fruits and vegetables, sweets and olives, and all kinds of spices and teas. You can enjoy one of the market's many restaurants, shop for produce, spices, or sweets, or just browse the ordered chaos of the place.

One of the most interesting things about the *shuk* in Jerusalem is the mixture of people, ranging from the locals who eagerly elbow their way to the vendors and the tourists who wander around taking photographs.

The secret to enjoying the *shuk* is deciding what type of experience you want. The most intense time and day of the week is 11am-3pm on Friday. The level of activity reaches a fever pitch as closing time gets closer and vendors want to sell more goods and shoppers want to buy their last items before the weekend.

The most low-key time to visit is generally any weekday before about 10:30am. You will have plenty of space to move about and enjoy the market without worrying about battling the crowds. You won't get many deals, though. The best deals are cut closest to closing time.

Later in the day, especially on Thursdays and Fridays, you can find all kinds of interesting characters in the main alley that runs through the market and is outdoors. You will likely see some characters here that are fixtures, including the man who takes photographs and sells them, and college kids or tourists who sit down in the middle of the pathway to drink beer and hang out. There is also often live music. It's just lovely, colorful chaos.

sausage for sale in Machane Yehuda Market

A main street leading into Jerusalem's heart is **King George Street,** significant for orienting yourself toward the Old City, City Center, West Jerusalem and East Jerusalem. The street is filled with shops of all kinds from electronics to clothing to food, and nearly every side street has additional shopping, hair salons, and restaurants.

Tolerance (Zion) Square

Shopping in City Center rotates on the axis of **Tolerance Square,** which runs between **King George Street** and **Yafo Street** and is at the foot of both **Ben Yehuda Street** and **Yoel Moshe Salomon** pedestrian malls. The square's name was changed in 2016 to honor the victim of a stabbing attack at Tel Aviv's annual gay pride parade. All of these shopping areas are mostly shut down for Shabbat and Jewish holidays, with the exception of a couple of restaurants. Much of the shopping in the area is limited to a few types of stores that sell souvenirs and Judaica, embroidered *kippot* and T-shirts, camera equipment, electronics and housewares, and local brands of clothing and shoes.

At the top of Tolerance Square, check out **The Book Gallery** (6 Schatz St. at corner of 26 King George St., tel. 02/623-1087, www.bookgallery.co.il, 9am-7pm Sun.-Thurs., 9am-2pm Fri.), the largest secondhand bookstore in Israel. It includes two floors with a separate section for old and rare books and a large basement.

Nahalat Shiva

Small and mostly stocked with books and materials in French, **Vice-Versa** (1 Shim'on Ben Shetach St., tel. 02/624-4412, www.viceversalib.com, 9am-6pm Sun.-Thurs., 9am-1:30pm Fri.) is a sweet shop with a warm atmosphere that highlights the fact that Jerusalem has a subculture of French residents. Mostly fun for browsing, the shop does sell some gift-related items like wrapping paper and cards and also interesting items for children.

For a truly unique souvenir, **Gaya Games** (7 Yoel Moshe Solomon St. at the end of Shamai St., tel. 054/392-0115, www.gaya-game.com, 10am-10pm Sun.-Thurs., 9am-3pm Fri., 7pm-11pm Sat.) has dozens of unique wooden games and brain teaser toys. The cavernous feel of their Jerusalem store, one of numerous locations throughout Israel, caters to adult customers who are interested in challenging play. Their **Creative Thinking Seminars** (contact Galit, tel. 03/903-3122, galit@gaya-game.com) allow you to play with some of their games and engage in challenging your brain.

The Cadim Ceramic Art Gallery and Collective (4 Yoel Moshe Solomon St., tel. 02/623-4869, 10am-10pm Sun.-Thurs., 9am-3pm Fri.) is a small, charming gallery and shop that serves as the storefront for a cooperative of 15 Israeli ceramists, who also run and staff it. Objects are displayed in groups by artist and every purchase includes the story of the artist. Prices start on the affordable end and go up, and objects include functional pottery, decorative objects, sculptural pieces, Judaica, and jewelry.

Shopping in the Old City

Shopping in the Old City can be exciting or intimidating. In many cases, aggressive shop owners won't allow you more than two seconds to glance at their products before pushing you to make a purchase. It is also a notoriously expensive place for English-speaking customers, particularly Americans. Despite that, it's tremendously fun and great exercise.

a shop in the Old City

Be prepared in advance to do the dance of bargaining if you plan to buy something, which might include literally walking away to get the best price. You can bargain if you are confident, but the best bet for avoiding some serious unplanned spending is to decide in advance on your limit.

There are seemingly endless streets of shops and cavernous stalls that are open seven days a week, and they have very similar items. The stores fall mainly into the categories of jewelry, religious items, souvenirs, clothing, antiques, and food. Most visitors enter the Old City area from Jaffa Gate and turn down HaNotsrim Street, a narrow pedestrian street in the Christian Quarter.

A good approach to shopping in this area is to walk past vendors and stores, and only slow down if you are seriously interested in buying something. Otherwise you will spend a great deal of time extricating yourself from negotiations with shop owners.

Shops selling antiques and artifacts, including Roman-glass inlaid jewelry and other locally handmade items, can be found mainly in the Christian and Jewish Quarters, although such stores are scattered throughout all four quarters. Be very cautious when purchasing antiques. You will need the appropriate legal certificate to take the item out of the country, largely due to problems with grave robbers and theft of antiques from archaeological sites. Check with the information center about the proper documentation necessary or visit the Israeli Antiquities Authority website.

Most vendors are more than willing to take American dollars, and you can find nice scarves, sweets, and cute trinkets. One of the great advantages to shopping in this area is that almost everything is open on the weekend.

A relatively well-kept secret, **The Eighth Note** (12 Ze'ev Raban St., tel. 08/919-9555, www.tav8.co.il, 10am-6pm Sun.-Thurs.) is visible by the small, black-and-white sign on its storefront. This side-street basement store has a nice collection of Arabic, Greek, Turkish, and other Middle Eastern CDs and DVDs. The friendly and knowledgeable sales staff will help you to listen to selections that you're interested in buying and will do their best to make sure you don't leave empty-handed.

EAST JERUSALEM

Renowned as an oasis of books in English on a wide range of subjects about Israel, the West Bank, and the conflict in the region, **Educational Bookshop** (19 and 22 Salah Eddin St., tel. 02/627-5858, www.educational-bookshop.com, 8am-8pm daily) is a combination of two bookshops, a small coffee shop, and a space for events in English. The friendly, knowledgeable staff can help you find a book on nearly any subject, and it makes the perfect place to have a coffee and watch the bustle of East Jerusalem go by.

OUTDOOR MARKETS

Every Friday you can find vendors at the outdoor **Bezalel Art Fair** (Schatz St. and Bor Shiber Garden by the Mashbir, www.bezalelfair.co.il, 10am-4pm Fri.) selling paintings, wood crafts, textiles, jewelry, glasswork, special and unique handicrafts, and food. The lively fair consists of carefully chosen vendors to maintain an overall atmosphere and a varied selection of art and artistic displays. Staged next door to the historic campus of The Bezalel Art Academy, the outdoor fair also includes a tour at noon from Bezalel to City Center.

A popular stop before the weekend is the **Farmers' and Artists' Street Market** (12 Emek Refaim St., 10am-2pm Fri.) that includes vendors selling jewelry, ceramics, toys, food, and a wide variety of other items for very affordable prices.

SHOPPING MALLS
Jerusalem (Malha) Mall

The massive **Jerusalem (Malha) Mall** (Agudat Sport Beitar 1 across from Teddy Stadium, tel. 02/679-1333, www.jerusalem.azrieli.com, 9am-10pm Sun.-Thurs. and 9am-3pm Fri.) is reminiscent of a southern California shopping mall in its size, parking, range of stores, and dining options. With 215 stores, it is Jerusalem's largest and nicest mall.

Hadar Mall

Very easy to reach by bus or taxi, **Hadar Mall** (26 Pierre Koenig St., http://hadar-mall.co.il, 9am-11pm Sun.-Thurs. and 9am-3pm Fri.) is extremely convenient and sells everything from basic necessities to doctor services.

Sports and Recreation

Jerusalem's location in the mountains at about 2,500 feet means that even in the hot summer months it boasts a cool, soothing breeze in the mornings and evenings. This makes outdoor activities a common pastime, including visiting natural springs, hiking, biking, swimming, camping, and cooking out (which is practically a national sport). Many Jerusalemites enjoy taking long walks through the city's scenic (and often hilly) terrain. Playing soccer, having a picnic, or simply sitting and relaxing are common.

Sherover-Haas Promenade

A paved walking trail with fantastic vistas, the **Sherover-Haas Promenade** (enter off of Daniel Yanovski St. at Olei HaGardom St., tel. 02/626-5900, ext. 102, www.s-aronson.co.il, 24 hours daily, free, free parking) boasts fantastic views of East Jerusalem, the Old City walls, and the Judean Desert. The winding walk down the promenade is nearly one mile (there are stairs at different points) and full of native plant and flower gardens, quiet places to sit, and viewing pergolas. The bottom of the promenade is the edge of the Judean Desert.

Orson Hyde Memorial Park

The two-acre wooded **Orson Hyde Memorial Park** (Brigham Young University Mormonic Jerusalem Campus on Hadassa Lampel Rd., free) is known for its views of the Kidron Valley and the Old City. The park is named in honor of Orson Hyde, a prominent member of the Mormon Church who traveled in the Holy Land in the late 19th century.

Gan Sacher

At little over half a mile long, **Gan Sacher** (between Ben Zvi Blvd. and the Knesset, 24 hours daily, free) is easily the park with the largest expanse of open green space in Jerusalem. As a result, it is a staging ground for major outdoor concerts during the summer, and on national holidays it is covered with a haze of smoke from families cooking out. It is home to two play areas for children, basketball and tennis courts, soccer fields, a skateboarding park, a jogging path, and a set of tunnels that run under Ben Zvi Boulevard and have been used in recent years for graffiti by local artists.

Follow the woodland paths near the center of Gan Sacher uphill toward the Knesset and you'll come upon the one-acre **Bird Observatory** (tel. 02/653-7374, http://natureinisrael.org/jbo, 24 hours daily, free), run by the Society for the Protection of Nature in Israel. The observatory is home to the Israel national bird-ringing center (schedule online) and features a wildlife blind to watch the myriad wild animals that spend time in this richly preserved and fortified natural habitat. Try going at night to see nocturnal animals by moonlight.

Liberty Bell Park

A stunning canopy of purple wisteria can be found in the spring in **Liberty Bell Park** (crossroads of Keren HaYesod and King David St. down to the beginning of Emek Refaim St., 24 hours daily, free) at the eastern end. The western end of the park is home to a very accurate reproduction of the Liberty Bell (hence the name), and there are several different playgrounds, walking paths, basketball courts, and picnic areas. It also hosts festivals, performances, and fairs, and is home to the Train Theater.

Train Track Park

The nearly 4-mile-long linear **Train Track Park** (also known as Railroad Park, 24 hours daily, free entry, paid neighborhood parking) following the old Turkish railway train tracks from the cultural and entertainment center at the First Station to near Malha Mall is a singular glimpse into local life and architecture. The paved jogging and bike path is always busy, while a boarded walkway covering the old railroad tracks allows for more leisurely strolling. The park is filled with plants, flowers, and benches to stop off for a rest along the route. It also has easy access to numerous dining and shopping venues along the entire route.

Bloomfield Garden

Full of character and history, **Bloomfield Garden** (runs along King David St. from the base of Keren HaYesod St. to Elimelech Admoni St. and west to Mishkenot Sha'ananim St., 24 hours daily, free) features massive agave plants, the family tomb of King Herod, and the remains of an ancient aqueduct. A unique landmark on the southern end of the 17-acre park is a fountain with distinct bronze lions encircling it (the symbol of Jerusalem). At the north end of the park is the venerable artist colony and cultural center Mishkenot Sha'ananim and the little-known **Gozlan Garden,** a beautiful, small park with fountains behind the world-famous King David Hotel.

Wohl Rose Garden

Magical **Wohl Rose Garden** (Government Center opposite the Knesset, tel. 02/563-7233, www.jerusalem.muni.il, 24 hours daily, free, paid parking) covers an area of almost 20 acres and is home to about 400 varieties of roses on 15,000 bushes. The park also has a variety of charming nooks and crannies, including an observation point and an ornamental pool. It is adjacent to other major tourist spots, including the Supreme Court and the Israeli Parliament.

Train Track Park is full of interesting things to do and see.

Just on the edge of City Center, you will find the sprawling **Independence Park** (bordered by Gershon Agron St. and King George St., 24 hours daily, free), with some good places to sit and enjoy a picnic if you've been exploring nearby City Center. Its terraced landscaping is dotted with a waterway system of an artificial creek and pools and frequented by families, but is rarely crowded except for the rare outdoor concert or event. The American Consulate is just across Gershon Agron Street.

Jerusalem Botanical Garden

A trip to the **Jerusalem Botanical Garden** (1 Yehuda Burla St., tel. 073/243-8914, http://en.botanic.co.il, 9am-5pm Sun.-Thurs., 9am-3pm Fri. and holiday eves, 9am-5pm Sat. and holidays, hours and price subject to change for special events, adult NIS30, senior and child NIS20) includes exploring 30 acres of landscaped grounds that include a renowned bonsai collection and about 10,000 varieties of plants from Europe and North America. Inside the grounds of the garden you can ride the Flower Train or walk along leafy paths. It also includes an indoor tropical conservatory, plants of the Bible trail, an herb and medicinal plant garden, and an African savanna grass maze.

BICYCLING AND SEGWAY RIDING

A tour on wheels is a great way to see and experience Jerusalem, especially at night without the hot Middle Eastern sun beating down on you. Biking and Segway tours also allow you to cover more ground in a shorter time.

For those already comfortable on a bike, the **Jerusalem Midnight Biking** tour (departs from the Karta parking lot, tel. 02/566-1441, http://jerusalembiking.com, call for upcoming rides, NIS115, NIS230 with bike and helmet) offers exercise and a chance to socialize. The three-hour tour

Bloomfield Garden gives access to East and West Jerusalem.

covers an approximately a five-mile circular route and passes through the neighborhoods of Abu-Tor, Yemin Moshe, and parts of the Old City.

Gordon Active provides a variety of bicycle tours, including **Bike and Eat Jerusalem** (departs from Abraham Hostel at 67 Nevi'im St., tel. 03/765-9018, www.gordonactive.com, 10am Tues. and Sat., NIS220). The seven-hour tour goes on a fairly exhaustive route and includes passing through the historic center of the city, the Calatrava Bridge, the Knesset and Supreme Court, Valley of the Cross, Rehavya, Talbiyeh, the German Colony, the Sherover-Haas Promenade, Mishkenot Sha'ananim, Jaffa Gate, and the Russian Compound.

A popular way to experience Jerusalem for those who aren't accustomed to the hills, **SmartTours** (tel. 02/561-8056, www.segwayz.co.il, tours daily, NIS180-330 pp) offers a variety of tours that allow you to see much of the city without getting worn out or stuck in traffic.

A new **bike share rental** program sponsored by the city set to launch in 2016 will initially include about 500 bicycles at 15 stations, largely in and around City Center.

HIKING AND WALKING

For very serious walkers, the **Jerusalem Trail** (www.jerusalemtrail.com) forms a circular route about 26 miles long through the city. It is part of the larger **Israel National Trail** that runs from the north to the south of the country. The trail should be marked with blue and white or blue and gold signs along the route, but it is highly recommended to download a GPS map from the trail's website. Between Mount Scopus and Yad Vashem there are occasional markings.

Rehavya Park (off of Ben Tsvi St., 24 hours daily, free) has extensive trails that are easy to navigate with sturdy shoes as the trails are a bit rocky. The views of the Valley of the Cross and its monastery below are magnificent. Walking in this area is better suited for cloudy days or early evening.

The **Jerusalem Forest** (off Highway 1 just past Yad Vashem, 24 hours daily, free) affords several good places to take relatively easy hikes if you have a reliable, sturdy car that can handle the sometimes extremely rough and rocky roads that lead to the hiking trails in the forest. If you are persistent, you can even find a spring or cistern to swim in along the way.

TENNIS

The **Hebrew University** maintains 10 outdoor, flood-lit tennis courts and two multipurpose courts (1 Churchill St., Mt. Scopus, tel. 02/588-2796, http://overseas.huji.ac.il, www.cosell.co.il, 3pm-10pm Sun., 8am-10pm Mon.-Thurs., 7am-5pm Fri., 8am-4pm Sat., daytime court rental NIS20/hour, evening court rental NIS25/hour, racket rental NIS20, purchase three balls NIS30) as part of its Lerner Center at its Mount Scopus campus.

The **Jerusalem Tennis Center** (1 Elmali'akh St. near Teddy Stadium and Malha Mall, tel. 02/679-1439, http://israeltenniscenters.com, court rental

goods store, and a snack bar. Part of the Israel Tennis Center network, the
center has a special purpose and mission to help underprivileged and dis-
advantaged youth.

SWIMMING

There are several public and private pools in the city that can be accessed,
but some have a rather high fee. Check the hours beforehand because of
different hours for men and women. The **Jerusalem Pool** (43 Emek Refaim
St., tel. 02/563-2092, www.jerusalempool.co.il, 5:30am-8:45pm Sun.-Thurs.
with varying hours depending on the day, weekdays adult NIS55, child
NIS45, weekends adult NIS60, child NIS50) is an Olympic-size covered pool
with five lanes, a large outdoor kiddie pool, and a waterslide. The grassy
area near the outdoor pool and the locker room are both a bit run down,
but the location is extremely convenient.

The seasonal outdoor half-Olympic-size pool at **Beit Yehudah Guest
House** (Haim Kulitz Rd. 1, Givat Massuah, tel. 02/632-2777, www.byh.
co.il, 10am-6pm Sun.-Thurs. summer, NIS70) is in the hills of Jerusalem
right near the Biblical Zoo.

The **Leonardo Plaza Hotel Jerusalem** (47 King George St., tel. 02/629-
8666, www.leonardo-hotels.com, 10am-7pm daily, weekdays adult NIS55,
child NIS40, Sat. adult NIS70, child NIS60) doesn't include a kids' pool,
but there are lounge chairs and the pool is situated in a calming garden.

GYMS AND SPAS

The **Dan Jerusalem Hotel** (32 Lehi St., Mt. Scopus, tel. 02/533-1234,
6:15am-9pm Sun.-Fri. and 8:45am-9pm Sat., NIS80) has a range of facilities including a gym, Turkish bath, whirlpool bath, saunas, and indoor and
outdoor pools (in season).

The **Akasha Wellbeing Center** (11 King Solomon St., tel. 02/548-2222,
www.mamillahotel.com, call for hours and entry fees) is inside the Mamilla
Hotel and includes a state-of-the-art gym, luxurious lap pool, spa, health
bar, sundeck, and holistic classes.

Food

Restaurants, coffee shops, and other places to eat and drink in Jerusalem
tend to be grouped together. In some cases, the distance between these
groupings is significant, so it's best to always carry some water and a snack
to tide you over if you're out sightseeing. In places like City Center, there
are food-related establishments every five feet.

Although it seems as though the city completely shuts down from late
Friday afternoon to late Saturday evening for Shabbat, there is still a choice
selection of places to eat and drink if you know where to look.

CITY CENTER

Middle Eastern

Yemenite Falafel (48 Hanevi'im St., tel. 02/624-2346, 9:30am-9:30pm Sun.-Thurs., 9:30am-3pm Fri., NIS40) is a reigning falafel master, run by a second-generation cook who learned the tricks of the trade from his father.

Another extremely popular falafel joint in a very touristy area is **Moshiko** (5 Ben Yehuda St., tel. 050/535-6861, 9am-midnight Sun.-Thurs., 9am-2pm Fri., NIS50). Its bright sign with large lettering is easy to spot, and it is en route to numerous other tourist activities in City Center.

Contemporary

A charming and conveniently located Jerusalem institution, **Kadosh** (6 Shlomtsiyon HaMalka, tel. 053/809-1548, www.2eat.co.il/eng/kadosh, 7am-midnight Sun.-Thurs., 7am-4pm Fri., 1 hour after Shabbat-Midnight Sat., NIS50) is known among locals as a good first-date restaurant. Kadosh's floor plan is smallish, but its atmosphere exudes the charm of classic Jerusalem. Kadosh serves an excellent, hearty, Mediterranean, prix fixe breakfast that includes a variety of salads, omelets and eggs, fresh bread, juice, and coffee. They also have a good selection of tasty patisserie and *burekasim*. They can get very crowded, so service is sometimes slow, but the food and coffee are consistently delicious.

One of the few restaurants in the city that is open 24 hours a day and serves bacon, ★ **Zuni** (15 Yoel Moshe Solomon St., 2nd Fl., tel. 053/934-5582, http://zuni.rest-e.co.il, 24 hours daily, NIS60) is centrally located, has incredibly friendly waitstaff, and an excellent breakfast menu. Housed on the second floor, Zuni is decorated in rich, dark wood with an enclosed bar for smokers away from the main dining room. The restaurant offers breakfast, evening, and late-night menus with fare to accommodate the mood of the time of day. The late-night menu features several desserts familiar to a North American palate, as well as a good selection of seafood and pasta. The morning menu offers various combination breakfasts with coffee and juice included. The evening menu features items like mussels, grilled eggplant, risotto, and quiche. Every menu has the option to add—yes, you guessed it—bacon.

Meatburger Iwo (28 Hillel St., tel. 02/622-2513, http://iwos.co.il, 10am-3am Sun.-Thurs., 10am-7pm Fri., 10am-4pm Sat., NIS40) serves up hefty hamburgers, wraps, and grilled chicken sandwiches that are big enough to satisfy the hungriest of customers. They are also English-speaking, deliver, and have a convenient online ordering system. It's better for takeout or delivery, as the atmosphere is more fast food than restaurant.

Nestled discreetly behind a row of buildings and up several staircases in the popular tourist neighborhood of Nahalat Shiva, ★ **Tmol Shilshom** (5 Solomon St. through the back alley, tel. 02/623-2758, www.tmol-shilshom.co.il, 9am-1am Sun.-Thurs., 9am-3pm Fri., NIS55) is one of the best ways for visitors to Jerusalem to experience local culture. Housed in a 150-year-old building and famous as a gathering place for well-known authors to read their works in English and Hebrew, Tmol Shilshom has hosted famous writers including Amos Oz, Yehuda Amichai, David Grossman, and others. An interesting and unique feature is the café's completely separate rooms, with a small outdoor patio in between. Among favorite menu items is their Amanda salad, salmon filet in fig sauce, and cheesecake. Their coffee is also excellent, and the cool, cave-like atmosphere makes it the perfect place for a late-night powwow with friends or as a temporary escape from the midday sun.

If you know in advance that you are going to eat out while in Jerusalem and want to experience something that is seriously hyped by Jerusalemites, call in advance for a reservation at **Machane Yehuda Restaurant** (Beit Yaakov 10, tel. 02/533-3442, 12:30pm-4:30pm and 6:30pm-midnight Sun.-Thurs., noon-4pm Fri., 8:30pm-midnight Sat., NIS100). Run by three Jerusalem chefs, Assaf Granit, Yossi Elad, and Uri Avon, the food is prepared with ingredients brought in fresh daily from the *shuk,* and the dishes are designed to reflect the character of each chef. The menu changes on a daily basis, and the kitchen is open for viewing. The general atmosphere of the place is rustic nouveau, which means your food might be served in a jar or on a cutting board, but the dishes are seriously delicious. In the evening, the small place is packed with tables and gets progressively louder and rowdier until you feel like you're in a club. It's not the place to go for a quiet, intimate dinner.

French

The lovely Shim'on Ben Shetach Street is home to cluster of upper-crust bistros with sidewalk dining, including ★ **Dolphin Yam** (9 Shim'on Ben Shetach St., tel. 02/623-2272, 11am-midnight daily, NIS60-100), one of the best known seafood restaurants in the city. It emphasizes serving moderately priced nonkosher seafood ranging from Israeli favorites to more commonly known items

Tmol Shilshom restaurant and café

Restaurants and Cafés Open on Shabbat

From late Friday afternoon to late Saturday evening, if you don't have some insider information, you'll find it difficult to go out for a meal because most places are closed. Scattered throughout the city are some outstanding nonkosher establishments that do stay open. You just have to know where to look.

CITY CENTER AND VICINITY OF THE OLD CITY

This is where most of the open places are concentrated. The Old City is always open, so restaurants are always available.

- **Austrian Hospice Café** (Old City near Damascus Gate, 37 Via Dolorosa, tel. 02/626-5800, www.austrianhospice.com)

- **Barood** (31 Jaffa St. in Feingold Courtyard, tel. 02/625-9081)

- **Blue Dolphin** (7 Shim'on Ha'tsadik St., tel. 02/532-2001)

- **Chakra** (41 King George St., tel. 02/625-2733, www.chakra-rest.com/en)

- **Dublin Irish Pub** (4 Shamai St., tel. 057/944-3740, http://dub.rest-e.co.il)

- **Focaccia Bar** (4 Rabi Akiva St., tel. 057/944-3123, bar.focaccia.co)

- **Lavan at the Cinematheque** (11 Hebron Rd., tel. 02/673-7393)

- **Link** (3 Hama'alot St., tel. 053/809-4510, www.2eat.co.il/eng/link)

- **Meatburger Iwo** (28 Hillel St., tel. 02/622-2513, http://iwos.co.il)

- **Notre Dame Roof Top Wine and Cheese Restaurant** (3 Paratroopers Rd., tel. 02/627-9111, www.notredamecenter.org)

- **YMCA Three Arches** (26 King David St., tel. 02/569-2692, http://ymca.org.il)

like bass. The menu also includes an array of meat and pasta dishes prepared in the style of French cuisine. Seafood soup, appetizers, and entrées make for seafood dishes for every taste. There are also some vegetarian options.

A refined fine dining atmosphere with indoor and outdoor seating can be found at **Gabriel's** (7 Shim'on Ben Shetach St., tel. 02/624-6444, www.gabriel-jerusalem.co.il, noon-5pm and 7pm-midnight Sun.-Thurs., noon-3pm Fri., NIS130), home to a nice selection of delicate, artistic dishes of meat and fish at this kosher restaurant. Some more unique menu items include the Chinese five spice duck breast and confit and a lamb slider bruschetta.

Although the Pontifical Institute Notre Dame of Jerusalem Center is a massive building in the center of the city, you could easily pass the outer walls without noticing it. Set back from the road behind a security gate, the institute is home to the **Roof Top Wine and Cheese Restaurant** (3 Paratroopers Rd., tel. 02/627-9111, www.notredamecenter.org,

- **Zuni** (15 Yoel Moshe Solomon, 2nd Fl., tel. 053/934-5582, http://zuni.rest-e.co.il)

EAST JERUSALEM
Most places in East Jerusalem are open, but it can be a bit trickier to navigate than West Jerusalem. The following are a couple of recommendations on the seam between east and west.

- **American Colony** (1 Louis Vincent St., tel. 02/627-9777, www.americancolony.com)

- **Askadinya Restaurant Bar** (11 Shim'on Ha'tsadik St., tel. 02/532-4590)

- **Pasha's Restaurant** (13 Shimon Siddiq in Sheikh Jarrah, tel. 02/582-5162, www.pashasofjerusalem.com)

WEST JERUSALEM
This area has slim, but quality, pickings.

- **Café Paradiso** (36 Keren HaYesod St., tel. 02/563-4805, http://cafparadiso.rest-e.co.il)

- **The Culinary Workshop** (28 Hebron Rd. in the JVP Media Quarter, tel. 053/934-4990, http://hasadna.rest-e.co.il)

- **Landwer Café** (4 David Remez St., tel. 02/587-7988, www.landwercafe.co.il)

- **P2 Pizzeria** (36 Keren HaYesod St., tel. 02/563-5555)

- **Scottish Guesthouse Restaurant** (1 David Remez St., tel. 02/673-2401, www.scotsguesthouse.com)

5pm-midnight Mon.-Thurs., noon-midnight Fri.-Sun., reservations recommended, NIS70), which offers outdoor dining on a beautiful rooftop terrace overlooking the city. The menu features 40 types of imported cheese and a large selection of wines from all over the world, including Notre Dame's private label wine. For something beyond cheese and drinks, the dinner menu offers a range of meat and potato dishes with salads.

Italian
For some authentic Italian fare, try **Topoleone** (62 Agripas St., tel. 02/622-3466, www.topolino.biz, 8am-11pm Sun.-Thurs., 8am-2:30pm Fri., NIS60), known for its superior service (waitstaff will bend over backward to accommodate you) and its variety of world-class pasta dishes. A note for those seeking a kosher establishment: the owners do not have a kosher certificate but claim that they serve strictly kosher food.

Headed by world-class chef Michael Katz, **Trattoria Haba** (119 Yafo Street, tel. 02/623-3379, www.haba.co.il, 7am-midnight Sun.-Thurs., 7am-3pm Fri., NIS60) occupies prime territory on the edge of the *shuk* facing busy Yafo Street. The kosher milk establishment serves a huge array of wonderful breads, pasta, meat, and vegetable dishes. Cheese plays a supporting role in many of Haba's entrées, including for cuts of meat. The atmosphere is bright and sunny with counter space facing Yafo Street in the front and outdoor garden seating facing the *shuk* in the back.

Pub Fare and Burgers

Part of a chain of pubs across Israel, **Mike's Place** (33 Yafo St., tel. 02/502-3439, www.mikesplacebars.com, 11am-last customer Sun.-Thurs., 11am-3pm Fri., NIS55) has a sports bar atmosphere. Unique on the menu is an offering of a variety of Mexican food favorites, which is next to impossible to find in Jerusalem. They also serve a wide variety of hamburgers, sandwiches, barbecue items, pizza, and salad.

Beyond popular for its hamburgers, **Josef** (123 Agripas St., tel. 053/936-7983, 11am-1am Sun.-Thurs., 11am-3pm Fri., 7pm-2am Sat., NIS45) serves up a selection of generous burgers prepared in a style that will satisfy the North American stomach. The interior has a warm pub atmosphere and is inviting and well lit. In addition to the standard burger and fries options, the menu also features modern touches such as gluten-free buns and vegan and veggie burgers. A modest selection of beer, liquor, and wine is also available.

More on the refined end for a pub, **O'Connell's** (3 Shim'on Ben Shetach St., tel. 02/623-2232, 6pm-last customer Sun.-Thurs., NIS50) Irish pub and restaurant has 12 beers on tap including Guinness, over 40 types of whiskey, and menu selections that include hamburger sliders, salad, wraps, and a lamb burger. The house specialty is fish-and-chips.

Dublin Irish Pub (4 Shamai St., tel. 057/944-3740, http://dub.rest-e.co.il, 5pm-3am Sat.-Thurs., 5pm-5am Fri., NIS50) is impossible to miss if you find yourself wandering in the vicinity of Tolerance Square. With its huge trademark painting of a toucan drinking a Guinness beer on a black background, Dublin is very bold about its presence. Inside there is a similar vibe, with a spacious floor plan that features solid wooden chairs and booths, a huge bar, and TVs for sports games. The menu features stock pub items like hamburgers, pizza, sandwiches, desserts, and a large snack menu to go with their huge bottled and draft beer list. Cocktails and every kind of hard liquor you could want are also available.

In a setting that is just right for a quiet lunch in a serene atmosphere seven days a week, **Link** (3 Hama'alot St., tel. 053/809-4510, www.2eat.co.il/eng/link, 11am-midnight Sun.-Thurs., 10am-midnight Fri.-Sat., NIS60) is fronted by a spacious wooden deck for outdoor seating and a lovely greenhouse-like interior with trees growing through the roof. The hamburger is one of the tastiest and most affordable options on the menu, but Link also serves a nice selection of fish and chicken dishes, calamari rings, fish-and-chips, and some Middle Eastern-style dishes.

Jerusalem's Restaurant Culture

Dining out in Jerusalem is a fun diversion and there are some genuinely wonderful gastronomic experiences to be had, but deciphering the unique rules of Jerusalem restaurants is a challenge. Here is a basic primer.

- **Closed for Shabbat:** This means several things, chief among them that they are likely kosher and close sometime on Friday afternoon anywhere between 3pm-5pm depending on the time of year. This type of restaurant often reopens on Saturday evening about 1-2 hours after Shabbat is over (when it is dark enough to see a few stars). The times vary a bit by season, but Shabbat is from sundown on Friday evening until Saturday evening; precise time calculators are available online.

- **Check:** You will never, ever get your bill in a restaurant in Jerusalem, or Israel for that matter, until you ask for it.

- **Coffee Shops:** Due to the strength of several national chain cafés that also serve as coffee shops, the presence of simple coffee shops or espresso stands is nonexistent. You can get a good latte (or cappuccino as locals call them) almost anywhere, though. Ironically, the best coffee is not served in the chain cafés.

- **Business Hours:** Security complications in this region have impacted business hours of establishments with the related decline in customers. Advertised business hours can sometimes be inaccurate; it is best to call in advance to confirm.

- **Kosher:** The kosher system dictates keeping dairy and meat separate, and kosher restaurants serve either milk or meat (meat includes fish). Kosher certification is officially issued by a governing Rabbinate and has degrees of strictness. In laymen's terms, it means you cannot get a cappuccino or real ice cream in a kosher meat restaurant.

- **Restrooms:** A cup with handles next to the restaurant's bathroom sink is for religious hand washing (not drinking) and means you are in a kosher establishment. Some places will have a special sink with a cup in the main dining area of the restaurant.

- **Security:** Watch out for the security fee that some places tack onto your bill. The practice has largely gone out of practice in recent years and it is only a few shekels when used, but you can ask to have it removed if you do spot a strange charge on your bill.

- **Service:** It is not unusual to have no specified waiter or waitress, especially if you are in a busy place. Feel free to call on any staff member you see.

- **Tipping:** The tip is almost never included in the bill, and there will be a large note in English on the bottom of your bill indicating "service is not included." A standard tip is about 15 percent.

- **Water:** There is a major shortage of water in this part of the world, so you have to request tap water and usually you have to request refills as well. A bottle of tap water is always free.

- **Wi-Fi:** Almost every single restaurant and coffee shop in Jerusalem has free wireless Internet. Just ask for the code if you need it.

El Gaucho (22 Yosef Rivlin St., down the alley, tel. 02/624-2227, www.el-gaucho.co.il, noon-midnight Sun.-Thurs., 12:30pm-3:30pm Fri., NIS110) is an upscale restaurant hidden in a back alley that serves an array of cuts of South American beef and a variety of wines. One of seven other El Gaucho restaurants throughout Israel, the interior of the Jerusalem location feels like a calm and inviting cave. The menu features items like *asado* (grilled steak), prime rib, baked potatoes, and meat skewers. They also have a dessert of the day and a children's menu.

To satisfy a meat craving, try **La Boca** (8 Shlomzion Hamalka St., tel. 053/944-2798, http://laboca.rest-e.co.il, noon-last customer Sun.-Thurs., 11:30am-6pm Fri., 8:30pm-last customer Sat., NIS90) for a menu featuring anything to do with meat, including rump steak, chili con carne, as well as some chicken and liver dishes. Self-described as Latin fusion, La Boca presents surprising takes on a wide variety of meat dishes prepared in the South American style.

Cafés and Coffee Shops

Café de Paris (1 Ben Maimon St., tel. 02/566-5126, www.joe.co.il, 8am-11:30pm Sun.-Thurs., 8am-4pm Fri., NIS55) is a relative newcomer to the Jerusalem restaurant scene. Situated just off a main road and easy to reach by a short bus or taxi ride from City Center, Café de Paris is popular for its breakfast menu and regional egg and tomato *shakshuka* dish. It is also favored for its relaxed, casual atmosphere and delicious European dishes cooked with a Mediterranean flair.

Café Mizrachi (12 Hashezif St. in Machane Yehuda, tel. 02/624-2105, 7am-10pm Sun.-Thurs., 7am-2pm Fri., NIS40), whose full name in Hebrew translates to "everything for the baker and coffee too," is a small café tucked into the *shuk*. The inviting shop has indoor and outdoor (under cover) seating, and in addition to food and coffee, it sells items for the home baker. The dairy menu includes sandwiches, salads, soup, and baked goods. It is popular and usually crowded.

The perfect place to stop off for dessert, **Babette Café** (16 Shamai St. at Yoel Moshe Solomon St., tel. 02/625-7004, 4pm-2:30am Sun.-Thurs., 11am-3pm Fri., NIS30) is one of the coolest little hangouts in City Center; little being the operative word. It's easy to overlook their cramped seating arrangements when you get your hands on one of their famous waffle dessert combinations with chocolate and whipped cream.

The draw to the **YMCA Three Arches** (26 King David St., tel. 02/569-2692, http://ymca.org.il, 7am-11pm daily, NIS50) restaurant is largely about the setting. It is the perfect place to enjoy a peaceful, shaded afternoon coffee on the YMCA building's massive veranda. The large front lawn and trees face the splendid King David Hotel, and you're a good distance the street. The menu is limited to a few pasta and egg items later in the day, but there is a daily breakfast buffet (7am-10am).

Near Zion Gate

At the juncture of the old Roman city's center and the current end of the partially renovated Cardo is a cavernous Arab restaurant with multiple names, but most easily located by its large sign outside the southern entrance that says **Heart of the Old City** (end of Cardo, tel. 02/627-3408, 8am-8pm daily, NIS35). The restaurant staff is friendly and serves up basic dishes of falafel, hummus, shwarma, and the like. It is also known as Afandi Restaurant.

Montefiore (Yemin Moshe St., below the windmill, tel. 02/623-2928 or 057/943-8439, http://montefiore.rest-e.co.il, 8am-midnight Sun.-Thurs., 8am-3pm Fri., 7pm-midnight Sat., NIS90) is a fine dining Italian restaurant with a menu that includes seafood such as salmon and also offers pasta and pizza. The establishment's main draw is its proximity to both the Old City and to the Jerusalem Cinematheque in the adjacent Mishkenot Sha'ananim complex. Outdoor balcony seating overlooks the Valley of Hinnom and has a nice view of the Old City.

Near Jaffa Gate

Inside Jaffa Gate's David Street, just east of the Church of St. John the Baptist, is Muristan Street, which has a row of several cafés and small eateries, many of which specialize in freshly squeezed juice drinks. Their hours vary depending on how many customers they have, but the general hours of these eateries are 9am-8pm daily. **Geo's Espresso Bar** (Muristan St. row of sidewalk cafés near the Church of the Holy Sepulchre, NIS20-75) serves chicken dishes, hummus plates, sandwiches, salads, falafel, and kebabs.

Jerusalem Pizza (end of Muristan St., 8am-8pm daily, NIS30) serves pizza at a storefront reminiscent of New York City, with a few guys behind a counter dishing up slices.

Na'aman Old City Coffee Shop (Muristan St., NIS55) looks pleasant as you pass by, and the menu includes *labaneh* (strained yogurt) plates, hot and cold drinks, sandwiches, and salads, but they encourage customers to pay rather high prices in U.S. dollars and the quality of the food leaves quite a lot to be desired.

The Armenian Tavern (79 Armenian Orthodox Patriarchate Rd., turn right at the Tower of David and restaurant is downstairs, Armenian Quarter, tel. 02/627-3854, 11am-10:30pm Tues.-Sun., NIS50) serves meat dishes with special touches like mint and grape leaves. The interior is what charms most customers the most, though, with its arched ceilings dating to the Crusader period and an indoor fountain.

If you exit from Jaffa Gate and take the stairs down to Mamilla, you will find a variety of places to eat, most of which are domestic chains and are often extremely crowded, particularly on Fridays. But **Roladin** (Mamilla Ave., tel. 02/623-1553, www.roladin.co.il, 7:30am-11pm Sun.-Thurs., 7:30am-3pm Fri., NIS40) bakery and café is always hopping, and for good reason. Its selection of sweet treats are prepackaged to be easily taken out, and they are the main draw for customers, even though a typical selection of egg dishes, sandwiches, and pasta can also be had. During Hanukkah, Roladin customers flock to buy their doughnuts (a traditional Hanukkah treat), which have earned a reputation for being the best in the city. The view of the city with both indoor and outdoor seating is fantastic.

Near Damascus Gate

The **Wiener Kaffe Haus** (37 Via Dolorosa, tel. 02/626-5800, www.austrian-hospice.com, 10am-10pm daily, NIS40) is a well-kept secret housed on the ground floor of the Austrian Hospice, one story above the Old City streets. The café has ample indoor seating and an expansive outdoor terrace under a canopy of trees. Wrapped around the building is a veranda with more seating, and there are several additional tables and chairs on more secluded vestibules raised above the patio. The limited menu includes a selection of items for a light meal including soups, salads, and toast. Tea in a pot, wine, and beer are also available and the Viennese apple strudel is a nice finish.

Near the Western Wall

Just before the security gate to enter the plaza for the Western Wall is a relatively good find for dining inside the Old City. **Between the Arches** (174 HaGay St., HaKotel HaMaaravi St., tel. 053/809-4584, www.2eat.co.il/eng/bta, 9am-6pm Sun.-Thurs., NIS65) serves a fairly standard fare of sandwiches, salads, fish, and pasta dishes but is extremely easy to find. The restaurant is located in an area that is part of a system of 13th-century tunnels, and you go rather deep underground to reach the dining room. The interior features an array of fish tanks and nice touches of decoration contribute to a relaxed atmosphere for a leisurely lunch.

EAST JERUSALEM
Middle Eastern

For a taste of home-cooked Arab food, **Pasha's Restaurant** (13 Shimon Siddiq in Sheikh Jarrah, tel. 02/582-5162, www.pashasofjerusalem.com, noon-11pm daily, NIS70) will pick you up from any Jerusalem hotel within 15 minutes of you calling them. Their sister establishment, **Borderline**, stays open until about 1:30am and offers a menu of *nargila* water pipes to smoke from for after-dinner relaxation. Pasha's menu includes traditional Arab fare of lentil and other soups, hot and cold appetizers, lamb dishes with mint, and a variety of international dishes such as beef Stroganoff.

Contemporary

The American Colony (1 Louis Vincent St., tel. 02/627-9777, www.americancolony.com, call for hours, open daily, NIS80) has several dining options for every day of the week in a beautiful five-star setting. Even if you're not a guest at the hotel, it's worth enjoying if you're willing to spend a bit more. Their Saturday brunch is extensive, delicious, and includes hard-to-find items like bacon. Options for dining include the Arabesque Restaurant,

The Courtyard, Val's Brasserie, The Cellar Bar, The Summer Bar, and The Terrace Café.

For a nice gastropub with courtyard dining, **Askadinya Restaurant Bar** (11 Shim'on Ha'tsadik St., tel. 02/532-4590, noon-midnight daily, NIS80) has created a blend of east meets west with meat dishes served with an Asian flair in addition to more common pasta and salad dishes. A specialty is the steak with a raisin and caramel sauce.

WEST JERUSALEM
Middle Eastern
Marvad Haksamim (Magic Carpet) (42 Emek Refaim St., tel. 053/934-5559, http://marvad.mapme.co.il or http://marvadhaksamim.rest-e.co.il, noon-11:30pm Sun.-Thurs., 9am-3:30pm Fri., NIS55), considered a Jerusalem institution, has been in business since 1948, on the eve of the founding of the country. Known for its Yemenite food and convenient catering services, the interior has the look of a diner with Middle Eastern touches, and take-out service is emphasized. The menu includes a variety of hummus dishes, Middle Eastern soups and salads (try the Moroccan carrot salad), as well as meat skewers and stuffed grape leaves.

Café Paradiso (36 Keren HaYesod St., tel. 02/563-4805, http://cafparadiso.rest-e.co.il, noon-1am Mon.-Thurs., 10am-1am Fri., 11am-1am Sat., NIS80) is an understated restaurant serving up creative Mediterranean and Middle Eastern dishes, including items such as grilled baby octopus, Thai lamb patties, and chicken livers on lentils. There's plenty of indoor and outdoor seating, and it is conveniently located midway between different tourism sites and parks, making it a great place to stop on the way to or from somewhere.

Contemporary
Nestled inside of the Jerusalem Cinematheque is **Lavan at the Cinematheque** (11 Hebron Rd., tel. 02/673-7393, 10am-midnight daily, NIS60), an ideal place for a quiet meal with a scenic view of the Valley of Hinnom and the walls of the Old City. Lavan is all about the atmosphere and the menu is a fairly generic version of what you can find all over Jerusalem, including pasta, egg breakfasts with cheeses, bread, and salad, and good cappuccino.

The Culinary Workshop (28 Hebron Rd. in the JVP Media Quarter, tel. 053/934-4990, http://hasadna.rest-e.co.il, 7:30pm-1am daily, NIS80) is very easy to miss during a trip to Jerusalem, which would be a shame. Tucked into the JVP Media Quarter, The Culinary Workshop has an enormous open kitchen, a multilayered floor plan with soft lighting and outdoor deck seating, and a limited, but extremely inventive menu. Dishes are prepared to give just the right balance of flavors, as with the artichoke à la Romana salad, which will win over anyone who isn't already a fan of artichoke. There is also a nice selection of steak cuts at reasonable prices, a rare find in Jerusalem.

Now in its new home at the First Station complex, local favorite **Adom** (4 David Remez St., tel. 02/624-6242, 12:30pm-2am daily, NIS80) has upped the class factor on their menu and decor to appeal to those who want something just on the verge of fine dining. Adom specializes in wine and international cuisine with French and Italian influences and features their take on a variety of lamb and filet mignon dishes.

Tucked away from view is **Colony** (7 Beit Lechem Rd., tel. 053/938-3942, http://colony.rest.co.il, 8am-midnight Sun.-Thurs. 8am-3pm Fri., 7pm-midnight Saturday, NIS70), known for its expansive indoor and outdoor floor plan and massive selection of wine, beer, and alcohol. The Colony is a favorite gathering place for foreign journalists and offers some fairly standard menu items, including schnitzel and hamburgers, but it also offers delectable crème brûlée and cappuccino. Housed in an old warehouse, Colony has tons of outdoor patio seating with a varied atmosphere that ranges from plush living room to tropical cabana. The waitstaff have a lot of ground to cover so need to be flagged down, but they are always accommodating and friendly.

A fantastic choice in combination with a visit to the Israel Museum is **Modern** (Ruppin through 11 of the Israel Museum, tel. 02/648-0862, www.modern.co.il, 11am-5pm Sun.-Thurs., 6pm-midnight Tues.-Wed., NIS85). The restaurant includes a huge patio area that is mostly used for private events, and a rather small but elegant interior. Known as a spot for frequent VIP sightings, including the president of Israel, Modern has a menu with a fairly standard selection of fish and pasta dishes. Their claim to fame is their Thursday night live jazz music and wine-tasting that starts at 7pm.

Halvrit Café at Cossell Jerusalem Sports Center (The Hebrew University at Givat Ram, across from the Bloomfield Museum of Science, 8am-10pm Sun.-Thurs., 8am-2:30pm Fri., NIS45) is one of the few places to have a light lunch if you are in the vicinity of Museum Row. Directly across the street from the Bloomfield Museum of Science, HaIvrit offers health-conscious food to complement the large number of customers coming and going from its sports center. Many of the choices on the menu are light salads and the like. There is nice, shady outdoor seating with a grassy area where kids can run around.

Asian

The flagship location of the popular **Sushi Rehavia** (31 Azza St., tel. 02/567-1971, www.sushirehavia.co.il, noon-11pm Sun.-Thurs., 11am-3pm Fri., NIS80) is one of several branches throughout Jerusalem. In addition to sushi, the restaurant also features delectable noodle dishes, Japanese-style grilled chicken, *gyoza*, and stir-fried dishes. The modern, Asian-style interior and atmosphere caters to the trendy set of Jerusalemites who are into a variety of gastronomic experiences.

Italian

P2 Pizzeria (36 Keren HaYesod St., tel. 02/563-5555, noon-midnight daily, NIS40) is a small, mostly pizza and some pasta restaurant that is open daily. The pasta is made on the premises in a large pasta machine at the front of the restaurant. The thin crust pizza is served up with high-quality ingredients and expert care. There's limited seating, including bar stools and outdoor chairs.

Seafood

Olive and Fish (2 Jabotinsky St., tel. 02/566-5020, noon-11pm Sun.-Thurs., NIS80) is conveniently located and features special seafood dishes as well as salads, chicken, and kebabs. Try the hot salmon salad or the St. Peter's fish filet. The interior of the restaurant is decorated with antique photographs of Jerusalemites through the generations, and is spacious and classy, with an indoor veranda.

Cafés and Coffee Shops

There is a lot of hype surrounding **The Coffee Mill** (23 Emek Refaim St., tel. 02/566-1665, www.thecoffeemill.co, 7:30am-11pm Sun.-Thurs., 7:30am-3pm Fri., 7pm-midnight Sat., NIS30) and some of it is deserved. The very small shop's walls are plastered with old *New Yorker* magazine covers, and the menu is bright and creative with pictures of most of the drinks and food, largely pastries. The late weekday hours make it a great place to stop in for a coffee after dinner nearby.

One of the most consistently excellent dining experiences in Jerusalem can be found at the ★ **Grand Café** (70 Beit Lechem Rd., tel. 02/570-2702, www.rol.co.il/sites/grand-cafe, 7:30am-11pm Sun.-Thurs., 7:30am-3pm Fri., 7pm-11pm Sat., NIS50) with its lovely selection of Middle Eastern-style food prepared in a style that appeals to the western palate. They serve generously portioned, mouthwatering salads and egg dishes, and beautifully done coffee and French-style desserts and pastries. The modern, warm decor includes plenty of outdoor seating year-round (in good and bad weather), and the waitstaff is unfailingly friendly, efficient, and welcoming. It is the perfect place to make the most road-weary of travelers feel at home and well-fed.

Grand Café

Accommodations

Most hotels, motels, and hostels in Jerusalem will accept payment in U.S. dollars, and they will often list their rates in dollars, rather than shekels for tourists. In general, Jerusalem hotels are on the expensive side. Many will offer a 5 percent discount for booking through their website.

Jerusalem has two main types of accommodations: those that are situated conveniently based on overall general location (such as City Center) and those that are situated as close to major tourist sites as possible (such as the Seven Arches Hotel at the top of the Mount of Olives). Beyond that, there are a wide variety of types of accommodations, including hostels, hospices, guesthouses, *zimmers* (bed-and-breakfasts), and kibbutz hotels.

CITY CENTER
Under US$100

Highly recommended by locals, ★ **Abraham Hostel** (67 Hanevi'im St., tel. 02/650-2200, www.abraham-hostel-jerusalem.com, US$29 d) is a medium-size hostel in the heart of Jerusalem that offers a range of rooms from single private rooms to a 10-bed dorm room, though private rooms are almost impossible to come by. The hostel was founded by backpackers and caters to independent travelers by aiming to be a one-stop location. The rooms are austere and sparsely furnished, but the hostel, which is the first in what is now a national chain, includes a wireless Internet lounge, common lounge area, dining hall, kitchen, laundry facilities, rooftop terrace, and a TV lecture room. All common areas are open 24 hours a day. The hostel also offers tours and activities.

US$100-150

If you're looking for luxury at an amazing price, check the **City Center Suites** (2 Hahistadrut St. on the corner of 13 King George St., tel. 02/650-9494, www.citycentervacation.com, US$136 d). It has elegant and modern apartments for short stays and long-term visits. Just at the base of Ben Yehuda Street, City Center Suites' rooms include studio, deluxe studio, and suite, and feature kitchenettes or kitchens, balconies, closet space, toiletries, and housekeeping service. The apartments have clean, modern lines and enough space for a comfortable stay.

The **Caesar Premier Jerusalem** (208 Yafo St., tel. 02/500-5656, www.caesarhotels.co.il, US$139 d) is a three-star hotel with 150 rooms and an intimate atmosphere. A standard room includes a mini-refrigerator, cable TV, breakfast, and wireless Internet.

US$150-200

The **Jerusalem Tower Hotel** (23 Hillel St., tel. 02/620-9209, www.jerusalemtowerhotel.com, US$155 d) is right in the middle of City Center, making it an ideal place to stay if you want easy access to the nightlife and a wide array of restaurants. The rooms are decorated in a very stark, clean modern feel with large, bright paintings on very white walls. Of the 120 rooms in the hotel, the rooms on the higher floors have views of the Old City. Amenities are very basic, such as wireless Internet in the lobby only.

Over US$200

The **YMCA Three Arches Hotel** (26 King David St., tel. 02/569-2692, http://ymca.org.il, US$229 d) is distinguished by a broad and picturesque veranda that wraps around the front of the historic building and a massive lobby with an arched and tiled ceiling that is classic Middle Eastern style. The hotel is part of a larger complex that includes a pool, gym and a restaurant with incredible outdoor seating. The rather austere rooms include free wireless Internet, garden views, and cable television. You can't beat the location on King George Street just a few blocks from both City Center and the Old City.

Popular, trendy, and smack in the middle of the city's action in Nahalat Shiva is **Harmony Hotel** (6 Yoel Moshe Solomon St., tel. 03/542-5555, www.atlas.co.il, US$338 d). One of the more popular downtown hotels for its blend of modern urban style in an ancient location, Harmony offers a happy hour in the hotel's English club business lounge with a billiards table, free computer for Internet use, free wireless access, a rooftop lounge area, and rooms with a mini-fridge, safe, and multichannel LCD TV. Part of the Israeli Atlas boutique hotel group, Harmony's 50 rooms are decked out with bright, modern bedding, rugs, and furniture.

The **Notre Dame of Jerusalem Center** hotel (3 Paratroopers Rd., tel. 02/627-9111, www.notredamecenter.org, US$330 d) is part of the massive, towering Pontifical Institute Notre Dame of Jerusalem that is situated just behind a hill from the Damascus Gate entrance to the Old City. There are 150 rooms, and the hotel caters to Christian guests making a pilgrimage to the Holy Land, though it welcomes guests of any faith. Amenities and facilities include a cafeteria, fine dining on the rooftop terrace, a chapel, and wireless Internet for an extra fee. The rooms are decorated in a somewhat plain manner, but are spacious and full of light and the room price includes breakfast.

Without a doubt, the ★ **King David Hotel** (23 King David St., tel. 02/620-8888, www.danhotels.com, US$600 d, includes large breakfast) is one of the most beautiful and elegant places in the city. Look for the massive table in the rich, lavish lobby where Israeli prime minister Yitzhak Rabin and Jordan's King Hussein signed their historic peace agreement in 1994. The patio and pool area behind the hotel make for a charming (and surprisingly affordable) place to have an elegant outdoor lunch. Some of the rooms include views of the Old and New City and balconies. All are richly appointed with sitting areas, modern furniture, and large-screen televisions. If you wander far enough behind the hotel, you will find the hidden gem, Gozlan Garden. The staff is exceptionally classy and accustomed to dealing with high-profile guests such as heads of state, but equally gracious to the common visitor.

The **Jerusalem Gold Hotel** (234 Yafo St., tel. 02/501-3333, www.jerusalemgold.com, US$240 d) is a classy, medium-size hotel with a bit of

European sass. The rooms are decorated with heavy drapes and rich tap-estries, and have extra-long beds, blackout curtains, and double-glazed windows for extra quiet. Guests can select their pillow from a menu, and video games and a laptop-size safe are available. The hotel is also close to several restaurants, shops, and entertainment venues.

Leonardo Plaza Hotel Jerusalem (47 King George St., tel. 02/629-8666, www.leonardo-hotels.com, US$450 d) is one of the easiest hotels to spot if you are in the middle of City Center. The hotel's tower overlooks the rolling green lawns of Independence Park. The 270 rooms are decorated in rich, bright colors, and there is an Italian restaurant on the premises. Guests have access to the new spa, seasonal pool, fitness room, and whirlpool tub.

Designed by renowned architect Moshe Safdie, the **Beit Shmuel Hotel and Hostel** (6 Shamai St., at the corner of 13 King David St., tel. 02/620-3455, www.bshmuel-hotel.com/en, US$205 d) has a distinctive glass dome covering the building's main dining area can be seen from Jaffa Gate and Mamilla. The modern, clean, bright interior of Beit Shmuel makes for a welcoming atmosphere, and the location is central to sights, food, and entertainment in both the Old City and New City. Small overall, but with a variety of accommodations, the guesthouse has 28 rooms for up to six people each, there are 12 hotel rooms for up to four guests each, and one apartment for a family or group visiting for a long-term stay.

The recently opened **Waldorf Astoria Jerusalem** (26-28 Agron St., tel. 02/542-3333, www.waldorfastoriajerusalem.com, US$450 d) is the height of luxury in the center of the city and a Conde Nast Best Hotel in the Middle East pick. The hotel's 223 rooms for guests exists alongside 30 luxury pri-vate homes built to specific tastes and needs of residents. Rooms feature Italian marble bathrooms, 46-inch flat-screen televisions, a private wet bar, an espresso coffee machine, free wireless Internet, and crystal chan-deliers. In addition to every possible amenity imaginable, the elements of each room can be controlled by the guest.

King David Hotel, behind the landmark Montefiore Windmill

Under US$100

The **Hashimi Hotel** (73 Khan El Zeit St., tel. 054/547-4189, www.hashimi-hotel.com, US$90 d) is situated in a building that is over 400 years old and at the center of the Old City. The modern interior features marble throughout and a rooftop terrace. The rooms in this medium-size hotel are quite bare, including bed frames made of wrought iron and rather thin mattresses. Wireless Internet, cable TV, and air-conditioning are included.

Just inside Jaffa Gate is **New Petra Hostel** (1 David St., tel. 02/628-6618, http://newpetrahostel.com, US$80 d), which offers free parking, a communal kitchen, and a rooftop terrace with panoramic views across Jerusalem. This small hostel has 42 private and dormitory rooms, a TV lounge, Internet, and free safety deposit boxes, as well as laundry service. The amenities and rooms are very bare-bones, so you are mostly paying for location.

Jaffa Gate Hostel (Jaffa Gate in front of David's Tower, tel. 02/627-6402, www.jaffa-gate.hostel.com, US$78 d) includes linens in the price, towels and hair dryers for rent, a place to park bicycles, a tour desk, luggage storage, currency exchange, and a postal and fax service. Dormitories and private rooms are available and are as simple and tiny as you can get, but they have a certain Middle Eastern atmosphere and charm. The hostel has evening movie screenings, free wireless Internet, *nargilot* (hookahs), a terrace area, and space for barbecues.

Although the accommodations are plain, the **Austrian Hospice** (37 Via Dolorosa, near Damascus Gate, tel. 02/626-5800, www.austrianhospice.com, US$85 d) is on one of the best locations in the Old City, and the hotel itself is lovely, clean, and very secure. The rooms and dormitories with bunk beds have only the bare minimum of amenities, and the small lobby is abutted by private, outdoor garden seating for guests and customers of the Austrian Hospice Café. Some of the staff are Austrian and efficient and

ACCOMMODATIONS

a room in the Waldorf Astoria Jerusalem

ACCOMMODATIONS

helpful. The rooftop view is one of the best in the area and a secret favorite spot among locals and those in the know.

Over US$200

Easy to miss in the hustle and bustle immediately after exiting the Old City by the Jaffa Gate and continuing to the end of the Mamilla shopping center, ★ **Mamilla Hotel** (11 King Solomon St., tel. 02/548-2222, www.mamilla-hotel.com, US$430 d) affords an incredible number of subtle charms for hotel guests and passersby alike. From its rooftop bar and restaurant to its wine bar, Saturday disco, live weekly jazz music in the lobby, and other varied offerings, the Mamilla is a bit like a world unto itself. The rooms are designed with sleek, efficient lines and accented with international touches such as Asian-influenced bathrooms and showers, and movable walls. Subtle touches of art throughout the hotel invite you to interact with your surroundings. Rooms have modern, clean furnishings, free wireless Internet, large screen televisions, and guests can use the Wellbeing Center and gym, swim in the luxurious indoor hotel pool or access the nearby outdoor David Citadel Pool. There is also a business center.

Connected to the Mamilla shopping center physically and historically, the Mamilla Hotel's owner had a direct hand in helping to revitalize the once-blighted area. There are some spots within the hotel that offer quiet places to sit and have a coffee. Try the outdoor patio adjacent to the massive dining room for a swing in a hammock seat and a view of the stars. The Espresso Bar, with a very calm, European vibe, is a lovely place to sit and work.

EAST JERUSALEM
Under US$100

Opposite the Old City's Damascus Gate, **New Palm Guesthouse** (4 Hanevi'im St., tel. 02/627-3189, www.newpalmguesthouse.hostel.com, US$70 d) offers package deals that include airport transportation. Private rooms are available, and there is free wireless Internet. Breakfast is available for an additional cost. The very simple accommodations at this small hostel also include free luggage storage, a common area TV, and a fully equipped kitchen. They also offer tours of Masada and the Dead Sea.

Close to numerous convenient amenities and the Old City, **Victoria Hotel** (8 Al Masoudi St., tel. 02/627-4466, http://4victoria-hotel.com, US$90 d) is a stone's throw from the central bus station, shops, and banks. The hotel has 49 recently renovated rooms, most with a balcony. Breakfast is included with the room, and there is free wireless Internet, 24-hour room service, cable TV, and hair dryers in the rooms.

Located on the famous and central Salah al-Din Street, **Capitol Hotel** (17 Salah al-Din St., tel. 02/628-2561, www.jrscapitol.com, US$99 d) has 54 rooms that include 24-hour room service, satellite TV, air-conditioning, a minibar, and laundry service. The interior of the hotel is very simple. The ground floor of the hotel features an idyllic garden dining area with a fountain and a large interior dining room.

The family-run boutique **Addar Hotel** (53 Nablus Rd., tel. 02/626-3111, www.addar-hotel.com, US$167 d) was rebuilt from a 19th-century building and features a plush, richly appointed interior. VIPs have been known to stay in this medium-size hotel that features a marble lobby as it is five minutes by foot to the Old City and near the British consulate. Rooms are equipped with marble whirlpool tubs, a balcony, French windows, a sitting area, free wireless Internet, and a safe. Some rooms include a kitchenette. The hotel restaurant has outdoor garden seating.

Well-equipped with an array of comforts and in a central location, **Legacy Hotel** (29 Nablus Rd., tel. 02/627-0800, www.jerusalemlegacy. com, US$170 d) has 49 rooms with sitting areas and hair dryers, a fitness center, and a restaurant with Middle Eastern food and an outdoor panoramic view of the city. There are also a bar, buffet, sushi bar, coffee shop, and garden restaurant.

A boutique hotel with simple modern luxury and design, **National Hotel** (4 Al Zahra St., tel. 02/627-8880, www.nationalhotel-jerusalem.com, US$199 d) is also close to East Jerusalem's shopping district of Salah al-Din Street. The generous-size rooms features large beds, and guests have access to free newspapers, hotel shops, a gym, and free parking.

The **Ritz Hotel** (8 Ibn Khaldoun St., tel. 02/626-9900, www.jerusalem-ritz.com, US$175 d) is a recently renovated 104-room hotel that boasts a lovely rooftop terrace dining area, a bar, 24-hour reception service, and satellite TV and free wireless Internet in the rooms. Each room has a personal safe, and the hotel is within easy walking distance to the Old City.

Over US$200

Known for its rooftop pool and outdoor restaurant with a panoramic view of the city, the **St. George Landmark** (6 Omar Ibn Al Aas St., tel. 02/627-7232, www.stgeorgehoteljerusalem.com, US$270 d) features 130 rooms and a Lebanese restaurant. Every room has free wireless Internet, an espresso machine, and tea and coffee machines. Many rooms also include balconies and views of the city.

The **Grand Court Hotel** (15 St. George St., tel. 02/591-7777, www.grand-hotels-israel.com, US$216 d) has 446 rooms, including family rooms and rooms that are equipped for people with physical disabilities. There is free wireless Internet and a pool and sundeck that overlook the Old City. There is also a dining room, garden terrace, and lounge bar in the hotel.

The **Olive Tree Hotel** (23 St. George St., tel. 02/541-0410, www.olivetree-hotel.co.il, US$300 d) is built around an ancient olive tree, which, according to legend, shaded pilgrims on their way to Jerusalem in ancient times. This large hotel has 304 rooms throughout eight floors and has been recently renovated. Rooms have over 50 international channels on the televisions, capability to dock laptops using the TV screen, and bathtubs. There is also a business center, babysitting service, and a large, inviting lobby with accents of Jerusalem stone.

Known as a gathering place for foreign dignitaries, high-powered business executives, and Jerusalem's foreign press, ★ **The American Colony** (1 Louis Vincent St., tel. 02/627-9777, www.americancolony.com, US$400 d) is still a posh meeting place and a world unto itself in the somewhat desolate surroundings of its East Jerusalem neighborhood. Full of quiet corners and lushly landscaped grounds, it is the perfect place for escaping from the heat and chaos of Jerusalem. Boasting three gardens, this five-star hotel includes an outdoor pool and sauna, fitness and business centers, a wine cellar restaurant, and a shop that sells antiques. The 93 rooms in four buildings offer a variety of luxurious accommodations with rich wood furnishing, arched ceilings, satellite TV, wake-up service, free toiletries, and some with sitting areas and balconies. The hotel has a decidedly Middle Eastern feel throughout the premises, from the beautiful tile flooring to the stone walls and overall decor. All of the staff are highly professional and speak excellent English, and the clientele tends to be seriously upper-crust.

WEST JERUSALEM
Under US$100

Hidden behind a stone wall in the heart of the historic German Colony is **St. Charles Hospice** (12 Lloyd George St., tel. 02/563-7737, pilgerhaus@netvision.net.il, US$90 d), a Christian guesthouse that caters to German-speaking pilgrims and features limited amenities. This small guesthouse offers rooms at a very low rate for the high-demand area it is situated in, and is just around the corner from some outstanding restaurants on nearby Emek Refaim Street. Also nearby is the Railway Park that stretches for miles, and the popular shopping and entertainment center at First Station.

The **Agron Youth Hostel and Guest House** (6 Agron St., tel. 02/594-5522, ext. 3, agron@iyha.org.il, US$98 d) is a 55-room hostel with air-conditioning, showers and bathrooms, TV and Internet, and even a minibar in some rooms. It caters to students and younger travelers and features basic, clean accommodations and the price of the room includes breakfast. The reception desk is closed for Shabbat, and cultural activities are offered on Sundays and Thursdays. The front desk sells discount tickets to some of the major sites in the city.

US$100-150

Tucked away in a neighborhood heavily populated with North Americans is the ★ **Tamar Residence** (70 Beit Lechem Rd., tel. 077/270-5555, www.tamarresidencejerusalem.com, US$144 d). Just far enough off the beaten path to be more affordable, but not too far to be inconvenient, part of Tamar is situated above the popular Grand Café. Long-term stays are also available, but book as far in advance as possible, especially for stays during the Jewish holidays. Each of the modern, bright rooms comes equipped with a kitchenette and plush furniture, and several also have an outdoor terrace. Most rooms have a separate living room area.

In keeping with the overall trend of guesthouses in the historic German

Colony, **Darna Guest House** (12 Hanania St., tel. 054/565-7001 or 054/227-2370, http://bnb.co.il/darna, US$105 d) offers three different locations with furnished apartments in central locations around the neighborhood. A member of the Home Accommodation Association of Jerusalem, Darna offers flexible rates for long stays with advance inquiries. The nicely furnished apartments include all the amenities of home and some include bonus features like outdoor patios.

Just at the entrance to the city is the **Jerusalem Gate Hotel** (43 Yirmiyahu St., tel. 02/500-8500, www.jerusalemgatehotel.com, US$150 d), in close proximity to the convention center and the central bus station, from which you can travel cheaply all over Israel. This large hotel has 298 rooms and caters to business travelers with its understated interior and proximity to the convention center. The rooms are a good size and simply decorated. Every room has wireless Internet, a safe, and hair dryers.

US$150-200

Avissar House (12 Hamevasser St., Yemin Moshe, near the Windmill, tel. 02/625-5447, www.jeru-avisar-house.co.il, US$180 d) has a small, but very nice selection of four do-it-yourself vacation suites. Though this type of suite is a specialty of the Jerusalem hospitality industry, Avissar House has something truly unique to offer: its location. Situated in the Yemin Moshe Artists' Quarter, Avissar is perfect for writers and artists, or those with artistic souls who like to be surrounded by beautiful flowers and the city's ancient stone. Each suite can accommodate several people, and features balconies and free wireless Internet, lush green plants, and comfortable furnishings. You can see the walls of the Old City, the Valley of Hinnom, and surrounding villages from the suites and it's a short, easy walk to the entertainment of City Center.

Part of the Little Houses in Jerusalem group, the boutique **Little House in the Colony** (4a Lloyd George St., tel. 02/566-2424, www.jerusalem-hotel.co.il, US$179) offers 22 rooms, and includes full amenities such as wireless Internet, shuttle service to and from the airport, 24-hour concierge service, and included breakfast.

The **Leonardo Inn Hotel Jerusalem** (4 Vilnay St., tel. 02/655-8811, www.leonardo-hotels.com, US$156 d) is a 200-room hotel situated at the entrance to Jerusalem near the Knesset. Some of the amenities include a spa and health club with sauna, whirlpool tub, and outdoor and indoor swimming pools. The light-rail has a stop in front of the hotel, which seriously ups its level of convenience even though it is not situated in the heart of town. The decor of the rooms is plain and simple, and the hotel caters to practical guests who are also looking for a certain level of comfort, but nothing ostentatious.

Hotel Yehudah (Haim Kulitz Rd. 1, Givat Massuah, tel. 02/632-2777, www.byh.co.il, US$200 d) is in the hills of Jerusalem, close to the zoo, Yad Vashem, and Malha shopping mall. The 129 rooms offered by the hotel include satellite TV, minibars, and many have a view of the gardens and the

Jerusalem hills. A swimming pool and café are also on-site. It is the perfect setting if you want to visit Jerusalem in style, but prefer to be a bit removed from the hustle and bustle of the city.

Over US$200

If you're looking for a more customized experience, **Jerusalem Harmony** (various locations, tel. 054/420-2198, http://jerusalemharmonystudio.com, Skype revamann, reva@jerusalemharmonyapartments.com, rates $200 and up) presents some interesting options. Accommodations have chic furnishings and include an array of deluxe guesthouses and vacation apartments fully equipped for longer vacations in prime spots throughout the German Colony; sizes vary from small to very large and can accommodate up to eight people. With writer Reva Mann as the property owner, the emphasis is on spaces that are conducive to fostering creativity.

Conveniently located **Prima Kings** (60 King George St., tel. 02/620-1201, www.prima-hotels-israel.com, US$217 d) is in an ideal location for visitors who plan on extensive sightseeing. The lobby feels a bit dark and small, but the 217 units in the hotel range in size from rooms to suites, some with balconies. There is a large and very useful information rack near the front door with a variety of tourist booklets and restaurant coupons for free. The hotel caters to observant Jewish guests with a synagogue on the premises and a Shabbat elevator. There is also a dining room, coffee shop, and business center, all of which are kosher.

The lovely **Ramat Rachel Kibbutz Hotel** (Kibbutz Ramat Rachel, Tzfon Yehuda, tel. 02/670-2555, www.ramatrachel.co.il, US$220 d) feels like a getaway in the city. The 165-room, four-star hotel is situated on the grounds of one of the oldest settlements outside the Old City walls in Jerusalem. Hotel amenities include an outdoor swimming pool, variety of room types, country club, kosher restaurant, money-changing services, and an active synagogue.

Information and Services

INFORMATION
Tourist and Travel Information

The hotline of the Jerusalem municipality is **106** (from out of the city call tel. 02/531-4600). It covers advisories and basic information for tourists. There are several places throughout Jerusalem that act as information centers. Some are better than others. In the Old City, the **Jaffa Gate Tourist Information Center** (1 Jaffa Gate, tel. 02/627-1422, 8:30am-5pm Sun.-Thurs., 8:30am-noon Fri.) is in a convenient location but has limited information and resources. The **Christian Information Center** (Jaffa Gate, tel. 02/627-2692, www.cicts.org, 9am-5:30pm Mon.-Fri. and 9am-12:30pm Sat.) is nearby and can also offer some help.

Outside of the Old City, near the City Center, the **Abraham Hostel Information Center** (67 Hanevi'im St., tel. 02/650-2200, www.abraham-hostel-jerusalem.com) has a 24-hour front desk and an information center that caters to independent travelers. The **Prima Royale Hotel** (3 Mendele Mocher Sfarim St.) has an extensive and very helpful tourist information rack just inside its front doors. Many of the tourism booklets include coupons for discounts on food and drinks.

Tourist Visas

Most visitors to Israel automatically get a three-month tourist visa at Passport Control depending on the country of the passport holder, which can be renewed at the **Jerusalem Ministry of Interior** (1 Shlomtsiyon HaMalka St., tel. 02/629-0231). A tourist visa can usually be extended for up to 24-27 months, but only in increments of 3-6 months and there is a fee of about NIS400 every time you extend your visa.

Media and Internet Resources

The **Jerusalem Development Authority** (www.jda.gov.il) recently partnered with the **City of Jerusalem** (www.jerusalem.muni.il) to create the **Official Tourism Website of Jerusalem** (www.itraveljerusalem.com). All three websites have useful information for tourism in the city, but the City of Jerusalem site has very relevant information on basics under its "visitors" section. Another helpful site is **Go Jerusalem** (www.gojerusalem.com) with its listings of everything from restaurants to tourist sites.

There are several locally broadcast radio stations, including 101.3FM and 88.2FM (not 88.0FM, which is a different Kol Israel network). A relay of the international broadcast Reshet Hey to shortwave overseas listeners can be had on an additional 10pm broadcast on 88.2FM. **IBA World Service Israel International Radio and TV** (www.iba.org.il/world/#) has an English news radio broadcast online and a TV broadcast at 5pm Sunday-Thursday on Israel Channel 3 (33 on cable) and 6pm Friday-Saturday. On Israel Channel 1, a 9-minute version broadcasts at 4:50pm Sunday-Thursday.

The official tourism website of Israel is **www.goisrael.com.**

Maps

The best place to find tourist maps in Jerusalem is through information centers or from the information racks that some hotels have in their lobbies. No matter which map you use, you will find many differences in street names and the names of sights. These are not errors of the mapmakers, but are due to the city's long history of places and streets being named by different groups, inconsistencies in translating words and names from Arabic and Hebrew to English, and sometimes there are political factors at play.

Holidays

There are several major holidays during the calendar year that draw visitors to Jerusalem from all over the world or greatly impact services and access if you are already in the city. The most impactful are Jewish holidays, and their dates vary slightly from year to year because they are based on the Jewish calendar. It's necessary to check a calendar to see when the holidays will occur.

The most major holidays are **Sukkot** (Oct.), **Yom Kippur** (Sept.), **Passover** (late Mar. or early Apr.), **Easter** (late Mar. or early Apr.), and **Ramadan** (one month around June-July).

Hospitals

There are several hospitals in Jerusalem: **Bikur Holim Hospital** (tel. 02/646-4111, www.szmc.org.il); **Hadassah Hospital** (tel. 02/584-4111, www.hadassah.org.il/Hadassa) at Mount Scopus; and **Herzog Hospital** (tel. 02/531-6875, www.herzoghospital.org).

Emergency Services

You can dial for emergency services from any phone by calling **Police,** 100; **Ambulance,** 101; **Fire Department,** 102; **Electric Company Hotline,** 103; and **Municipal Emergency Situation Room,** tel. 02/625-6202 (for information during emergencies).

SERVICES
Currency Services and Money Exchange

There are several "Change" stands located throughout the city that will change foreign currency into New Israel Shekels (shekels for short) and vice versa. Change offices are concentrated in and around Tolerance Square and in the German Colony and Bak'a. If you are in the Old City, a trustworthy and very easy to find money exchange office is **Abu Ghazeleh Money Exchange** (Old City at Damascus Gate, tel. 02/628-2479, 9am-6pm daily) just inside Damascus Gate to the right. The owner speaks perfect English and has been in business at the same location for 40 years.

Post offices (www.israelpost.co.il) cash foreign currency checks and traveler's checks. The official symbol of the post office is a red sign with white writing and an ibex leaping with its horns above the title of the post office. A complete listing of the post office branches in Jerusalem can be found on the post office website.

Banks are open 8:30am-12:30pm Sunday-Friday (closed for Shabbat and holidays), and some also open from late afternoon until evening. There are several bank branches in Jerusalem that change money, including the **Jerusalem Center Branch** (33 Jaffa St.), the **City Center Shamai Branch** (6 Shamai St.), and the **Old City Jewish Quarter Branch** (69 Hayehudy St.). Near Nahalat Shiva and directly next door to the Ministry of Interior is **Hillel Change** (1 Shlomtsiyon HaMalka St., tel. 02/623-0656), which operates under the supervision of the Bank of Israel.

ATMs

There are ATMs outside of most banks, and they take foreign bank cards.

There is a fee of US$3-9 charged by most banks for using their card at a foreign ATM.

Tolerance Square has two conveniently located banks with outdoor ATMs that take foreign cards. **Bank Hapoalim** (www.bankhapoalim.co.il) has red, blue, and white colors on its sign, and other branches can be found throughout Jerusalem, including in Emek Refaim across the street from Masaryk restaurant, in Bak'a downhill from the Sherover-Haas Promenade, and at the base of Tolerance Square where it meets with Yafo Street. The **Israel Discount Bank** (www.discountbank.co.il) has green and white colors and branches throughout Jerusalem.

Internet

Free wireless Internet (often without a password) is available almost everywhere in the city, particularly in restaurants and cafés. City Center has free Wi-Fi provided by the municipality.

There are also about 100 Wi-Fi hotspots in convenience stores adjacent to gas stations, and other spots are available at universities, colleges, museums, visitors centers, convention halls, marinas, tourism sites, and shopping malls.

Postal Service

There are more than 20 branch **post offices** (main branch at 23 Yafo Street opposite Safra Square, tel. 02/629-0676, www.israelpost.co.il, most operate 9am-3pm Sun.-Thurs., 9am-2pm Fri.) throughout Jerusalem. Check the branch for hours.

Transportation

GETTING THERE

Air

The airport closest to Jerusalem is the **Ben Gurion International Airport** (tel. 03/975-2386, www.iaa.gov.il) outside Tel Aviv.

Known as the de facto national airline, **El Al Airlines** (www.elal.co.il) has frequent flights to Tel Aviv from all over the world and provides kosher meals. Most major international airlines offer at least one flight a day to Tel Aviv.

There are several ways to reach Jerusalem from the airport if you are not staying at a hotel with a shuttle service. Jerusalem is about one hour by car from the airport, about two hours by train, and a little over one hour on the many frequent, convenient, and comfortable buses. Public transportation does not run during Shabbat (from Fri. afternoon through 8pm or 9pm Sat.), but it is possible to get a service taxi from certain locations during that time.

Be careful when planning a flight around Shabbat or on a major Jewish holiday. You will have a more difficult time reaching your final destination if you plan to arrive or depart during these times.

SECURITY CHECKPOINTS AND VEHICLE SEARCHES

Jerusalem is under ongoing threats from terrorist attacks, and it is not unusual to be stopped and questioned coming and going from a public place or to have your bag searched before entering a building. Metal detectors at building entrances are common. If you are in a car, the trunk might be searched, you might be asked for your ID, and you might be questioned. Refrain from joking with security personnel or saying you have a package given to you by someone else.

Train

Israel Railways (www.rail.co.il, NIS22.5) has a train that takes at least two hours from the airport to Jerusalem, and stops for at least 30 minutes between at a train change location. Once in Jerusalem, you will be a good 15 minutes from City Center and will need to go by car or bus to your final destination.

Share Taxi

Just north of Tolerance Square on Harav Kook Street is an unofficial way station for share taxis going to and from Tel Aviv and other locations. The cost is about NIS30, and the vans will not leave until they are full, so you might have to wait for a while. Check with the driver before getting in that they are going to your destination.

GETTING AROUND

Jerusalem can be tricky to maneuver if you take a wrong turn, particularly if you're traveling by car. It's highly recommended to go by foot or take advantage of Jerusalem's efficient bus system, ample taxis, and the light-rail train to get around.

Car Rental and Driving

Visitors to Israel are allowed to drive with their foreign license for up to one year from arrival in the country. As most street signs are in English, it is relatively easy for someone who doesn't speak Hebrew to drive in Jerusalem.

With three locations in Jerusalem, **Hertz** offices can be found in Givat Shaul, King David, and Romema. The King David branch (19 King David St., tel. 02/623-1351, www.hertz.co.il) is centrally located in the city, and you can get compact Suzukis and Hyundais starting at US$37 a day.

Budget (23 King David St., tel. 03/935-0015, www.budget.co.il) has a wide variety of car models, from compact cars to SUVs, and two locations in Jerusalem. Their main Jerusalem office is on centrally located King David Street.

The parking system in Jerusalem has some strict rules and some that you can break. For instance, you might see cars parked on the sidewalk or facing the wrong direction especially during the weekend or when spots are at a premium due to a crowd. One rule you break at your peril, though, is not feeding the meter. Red and white stripes mean no parking, blue and white stripes mean paid parking by a street meter, and gray is free parking. Other paid parking in certain neighborhoods or small lots will have a yellow and black sign with hours of paid parking; for these, you must buy a ticket and leave it in your car dash with the date stamp showing. These machines often take nothing but coins.

If you are going to be in Jerusalem and driving on a daily basis, Yellow gas stations sell an automatic pay-in-advance meter that you leave on the side of your vehicle. The meter costs NIS100 and you can pay for time on it as you go.

Taxis

Taxis in Jerusalem are white cars with a yellow light on the roof and are often BMWs. You can get almost anywhere in the city (without heavy traffic) for NIS50 or less. Drivers might offer you a fixed rate or simply not turn their meter on, but you can rarely beat the meter with a set rate. There is a NIS10 (about US$1.25) drop charge at the start of every ride, and an additional NIS5 charge for summoning a taxi to a hotel. There can be an additional charge for luggage, and some drivers might try to charge more for two or more passengers.

The legal fare system is 25 percent higher during Shabbat and holidays (sundown on Fri. until it is dark on Sat. night, usually about 8pm). Fares are also 25 percent higher at night, 9:01pm-5:29am.

Tips are not generally expected, but are always appreciated. If you need a taxi for a long distance, it is better to call and order a cab.

The light-rail train provides convenient and fast transportation.

Two reputable taxi companies in Jerusalem are **Rehavia Taxi** (3 Agron St., tel. 02/622-2444) and **HaPisga Taxi** (2 HaPisga St., tel. 02/642-1111).

Public Transportation

Jerusalem's city bus line, **Egged** (tel. 03/694-8888 or *2800 from any local phone, www.egged.co.il), provides service throughout the city and country. Within the city, it costs about NIS7 for a one-way trip. The Rav Kav ticket can be purchased and filled for multiple trips and works in both Jerusalem and Tel Aviv. Egged's bus 99 offers a panoramic tour of Jerusalem aboard a red double-decker tour bus with stops that you can hop on and off with a one- or two-day pass (NIS39). Bus stops throughout the city have a timed arrival chart for every impending arrival, but the bus line explanations are only posted in Hebrew.

The **Central Bus Station** (218 Yafo St., tel. 054/797-1147) is a typical transportation hub with several levels that also support shops and places to eat or get a snack. Bus tickets can be purchased at the information window on the second level or directly from your driver if you are paying cash. Bus seats are on a first-come, first-served basis, and people stand and sit in the aisles if the seats run out.

Overseas visitors can buy Israbus tickets, valid on all Egged bus lines and on the light-rail train. They are available at all branches of Egged Tours.

The **light-rail train** (tel. 073/210-0601 or *3686 from any local phone, www.citypass.co.il, NIS6.90) is a fast and convenient way to get around in certain parts of the city. It is the most convenient way, for example, to get from City Center to Yad Vashem. But the route is rather limited and does not include many major tourist sites. As it runs roughly along the old border between East and West Jerusalem, it is very convenient if you want to get somewhere in East Jerusalem. The ticket purchasing system is tricky, so leave extra time to get it right the first time.

Vicinity of Jerusalem

Not far from Jerusalem there are several enchanting and interesting places for a different perspective on the region. Visitors with an interest in history, archaeology, spirituality, and nature will find something to pique their interest. It is particularly recommended to visit areas outside of Jerusalem during Shabbat, as the majority of restaurants and sights remain open.

You can take a **taxi** to any of the locations outside of Jerusalem, but the fare will be very costly. A 20-minute ride will cost about NIS120 or more. A **rental car** is a good option, as all of the signs are posted in English.

HADASSAH EIN KEREM

If you're a serious art lover, it might be worth your while to take a major detour to **Hadassah Ein Kerem,** one of the leading research hospitals in the world, which is also home to the famous **Marc Chagall Stained Glass**

Windows (off of Route 396 near Ein Kerem, tel. 02/677-7111, www.hadas-sah.org.il), a series of 12 arched, stained glass windows surrounding the hospital's synagogue. They can be viewed for free just after entering the hospital lobby. Chagall called the windows his "modest gift to the Jewish people," and they were recently renovated. The drive to Hadassah through the Jerusalem forest is very scenic, and there are numerous other works of art throughout the hospital donated by the artists themselves or supporters. Nearby Ein Kerem offers several interesting sights as well as a variety of good dining and drinking options.

Getting There

To get to Hadassah Hospital, take **Egged** bus (www.egged.co.il) number 19 from Jerusalem's Central Bus Station.

EIN KEREM

About 20 minutes northwest of Jerusalem is the scenic valley village of **Ein Kerem,** believed to be the birthplace of John the Baptist, whose mother was the Virgin Mary's cousin.

Sights

One of the most popular tourist and pilgrim draws in Ein Kerem is **Mary's Well** (southern end of HaMa'ayan St., 24 hours, free), which Christian tradition says was a site visited by the Virgin Mary when she stopped here to drink from the spring. A 19th-century mosque can be seen above the spring.

The **Shrine of the Visitation** (southern hill facing the village at the top of the pedestrian extension of HaMa'ayan St., tel. 02/641-7291, www.custodia.org, 8am-noon and 2:30pm-6pm Mon.-Sat., NIS5) is a church with a

a section of the Marc Chagall Stained Glass Windows at Hadassah Hospital

facade on the front with a series of arches, a bell tower, and a painting of the Virgin Mary riding a donkey and accompanied by angels on the front outer wall. The two-story church has large color paintings throughout depicting biblical scenes. It is also home to a guesthouse run by nuns.

The iconic **Gorny Monastery,** also known as Moscavia for its distinctive gold onion domes that are clearly visible from the village, can be reached by taking a short hike up a steep, winding footpath. The 19th-century Russian Orthodox church is also home to a convent. The compound's buildings are closed to the public, but you can get an excellent view from the parking lot on HaOren Street next to Shibboleth Lane.

The **Sisters of Zion Convent** (1/2 HaOren St., tel. 02/641-5738, 9am-noon and 2pm-5pm Mon.-Fri., 9am-5pm Sat., ring for entrance, NIS2) is home to an archaeological garden and chapel.

The **Church of St. John** (Mevo Hasha'ar, tel. 02/632-3000, 6am-noon and 2pm-5pm daily, free) is built at the location where John the Baptist was believed to have been born. The church has a grotto beneath it with the remains of a Byzantine mosaic.

Food

Ein Kerem is a fun place to go during the weekend when not much is happening in Jerusalem. You can do a little sightseeing, take a stroll, get a drink, or have dinner and enjoy a leisurely coffee and dessert. The main concentration of places to get food and drinks is on two roads: to the end of HaMa'ayan Street and along the part of Ein Kerem Road 74 where it passes through the village.

Offering a nice array of chicken and beef dishes, **Charlotte** (25 Ein Kerem Rd., tel. 02/643-4545, noon-11pm Sun.-Thurs., NIS70) is perfect if you're in the mood for something grilled. Though they are one of the few places not open on the weekend, Charlotte has the unusual offering of goose breast skewers. All of their entrées are served with salad, and their interior is large and spacious with wood paneling and huge windows that give it the feeling of a cabin.

Brasserie (15 HaMa'ayan St., tel. 02/566-5000, www.2eat.co.il/eng/brasseriejer, noon-last customer Sun.-Wed., 10am-last customer Thurs., 9:30am-last customer Sat., NIS60) has a large patio on its second level for outdoor seating in good weather. The patio affords a nice view of the scenic setting. Serving seafood, including mussels and shrimp, the restaurant also has a good selection of steak, chicken, and French-inspired dishes (try the camembert croissant). Brasserie also has a nice liquor and wine selection, and customers can arrange a menu for wine-tasting. Four beers on tap are served, as well as an array of signature cocktails.

Karma (74 Ein Kerem Rd., tel. 02/643-6643, www.karma-rest.co.il, 10am-midnight Sun.-Wed., Thurs.-Sat. 10am-1am, NIS70) has a nice layout and very accommodating waitstaff. The menu is a fairly typical blend of pasta, salad, and meat selections with some delightful surprises. Try the taboon-baked flatbread covered with vegetables and eggs or the Druze-inspired appetizer platter, which consists of a thin pita overstuffed with lamb cuts, pine nuts, red sauce, tahini, and roasted eggplant. Karma also has enclosed veranda seating on the first floor and tons of balcony seating on the second floor.

Accommodations

The **Rosary Sisters Ein Kerem Guest House** (3 HaMa'ayan HaBikur St., tel. 02/641-3755, www.rosary-einkarem.com, US$90 d) is a small guesthouse run by nuns in the hills of Ein Kerem at the site of Sisters of Zion Convent. The rooms are small and simply furnished, and facilities include a reception area and a small dining room.

The **Sister of Sion Guest House** (23 HaOren St., Ein-Kerem D, tel. 02/641-5738, http://sion-ein-karem.org, US$80 d) offers a small selection of simple rooms with free wireless Internet for singles, couples, and families. All rooms have heating, but only some have air-conditioning.

Getting There and Around

To get to Ein Kerem, take **Egged** bus (www.egged.co.il) number 17 from City Center; it takes about 25 minutes (NIS12). Once there, the village is easy to navigate by foot and there is no need for a vehicle.

If you're driving, note that parking is extremely limited on the weekend.

HERODIUM

About eight miles south of Jerusalem is King Herod's palace-fortress, **Herodium** (south of Jerusalem and east of Bethlehem on edge of Judean

Herodium, the ancient ruins of King Herod's palace

Desert, tel. 050/623-5821, www.parks.org.il, 8am-5pm daily Apr.-Sept., 8am-4pm daily Oct.-Mar., NIS27). According to one historical account, he built it after winning a victory over the Hasmoneans and Parthians. The palace is 758 meters above sea level. The site contains extensive palatial ruins, including a living quarter complex, an ancient synagogue, and underground tunnels, and it can be accessed by foot.

Getting There

If you are venturing out to Herodium, you can go and return by bus, though you will also have to do a fair amount of walking. **Egged** bus (www.egged.co.il) number 266 toward Karmei Zur will get you close, followed by a 20-minute walk.

LATRUN

Latrun is an easy side trip off Highway 1 by car.

Sights

One way to cover a lot of ground in a short time is to see **Mini-Israel** (Latrun near Kahativa 7 Junction, tel. 700/559-559, www.minisrael. co.il, 10am-6pm Sun.-Thurs., 10am-2pm Fri. Sept.-June, 5pm-10pm Sun.-Thurs., 10am-2pm Fri. July-Aug., adult NIS79, child NIS59). The miniature theme park has 385 exact replica models on a 1:25 scale of Israel. The models are positioned among bonsai trees and miniature figurines of Israelis. There is also a 3D movie of Israeli landscapes, a restaurant and cafeteria, multimedia and play area for kids, and a new MiniMax aerial movie of Israeli sites.

Just off of Highway 1 is the **Latrun Monastery** (tel. 08/922-0065, 9am-1pm and 2pm-5pm Mon.-Sat., free), founded in 1890 and home to an order of silent monks up until the 1960s. The site consists of a large church and living quarters on the monastery grounds, garden, vineyard, and orchards. In late 2012, the monastery was vandalized by Jewish settlers angry over being removed by the government from their settlement. As you enter the site, you will find a shop selling Domain de Latroun wines, liqueurs, spirits, and olive oil and honey made at the monastery.

Getting There

To get to Mini-Israel, take **Egged** bus (www.egged.co.il) number 433 to Mishamar Ayalon Junction (NIS24). To get to the Latrun Monastery, take Egged bus number 403, 433, or 434, a 25-minute ride from Jerusalem's Central Bus Station (NIS16).

Abu Ghosh is a quiet Arab village just off Highway 1, famed for its hummus and other Arab delicacies. It's about 25 minutes northwest of Jerusalem.

Sights

Just outside of Jerusalem near the villages of Bet Nekofa and Abu Ghosh is **Ein Hemed (Aqua Bella)** national park (off the main Hwy. 1 from the Hemed off-ramp, opposite Kibbutz Kiryat Anavim and the town of Abu Ghosh, tel. 02/534-2741, 9am-6pm daily, NIS20), which was once used as a way station for Crusaders. You can still find the remains of a ruined Crusader farmhouse and a park with an olive press.

Food

There are several good options in Abu Ghosh for Arab cuisine, including hummus, falafel, and shwarma. Try **The Original Abu Shukri** (15 Hashalom Way, tel. 02/652-6088, 8am-8pm daily, NIS45), which gets its name from a dispute with another restaurant. The dispute is that one (nobody is sure which anymore) is regarded as having the best hummus in all of Israel. The interior of the restaurant is very simple and homey, and the dining experience is, like most hummus dining, without much fanfare. But the food is delicious and comes to your table quickly, the service is good, and there is free parking.

The Lebanese Restaurant (65 Kvish Ha-Shalom, tel. 02/533-2019, 11am-11pm daily, NIS30) is another favorite for hummus. The decor is spartan but the food is divine, and you are guaranteed to leave with a full stomach and money still in your wallet.

If you're tired of Middle Eastern food, you can find the **Elvis American Diner** (near the Neve Ilan gas station, tel. 02/534-1275, 7am-midnight daily, NIS80) in Abu Ghosh, serving up what are widely reputed to be some of the best hamburgers in the area. A large statue of Elvis is outside the building, and Elvis pictures cover the walls inside.

Getting There and Around

To get to Abu Ghosh, take **Superbus** (www.superbus.co.il) number 185 or 186, about a 40-minute ride (NIS25). Once you are there everything is within fairly easy walking distance.

For the gorgeous parklands of Ein Hemed (Aqua Bella), the Superbus 185 leaves from Jerusalem every hour. It's about a 30-minute ride (NIS22). Just get off at Beit Nekufa and walk for 10 minutes over the bridge that goes over Road 1.

The major hub for Superbus in Jerusalem is in East Jerusalem near Damascus Gate.

Background

The Landscape

You will often hear Israelis say that theirs is a small country, and it's true. The total area of the State of Israel is 8,630 miles, comprised mostly of landmass. At its widest it is 85 miles across and from the northernmost point to the southernmost point it is 290 miles.

GEOGRAPHY

Israel's western coast runs along the Mediterranean Sea, and elsewhere Israel is bordered by several other countries, not all of which can be characterized as friendly. In the north, its neighbors are Lebanon and Syria; on the east is the Hashemite Kingdom of Jordan; and Egypt is in the south.

The West Bank, a landmass of about 2,270 square miles, sits between Israel and Jordan; some refer to it as Judea and Samaria and others as the Palestinian Territories. To characterize the West Bank as part of Israel is a grave misnomer. The West Bank's three distinct divisions fall under the categories of A, B, and C: Palestinian Authority-controlled, joint Palestinian Authority and Israeli-controlled, and Israeli-controlled, respectively. About 60 percent of the West Bank is Area B or C, and there are 400,000 Israelis living there, including those who are residents of East Jerusalem.

The number of Arab residents of the West Bank is a matter of huge debate, but is usually cited as somewhere between 2.6 million and 2.7 million. Part of the dispute over accurate census numbers is due to inclusion of populations from East Jerusalem and Gaza. The majority (over 60 percent) of the country's 8.46 million people live in either the metropolitan Tel Aviv area or Jerusalem.

As for the West Bank's landscape, a major feature in the summer and autumn months is the silvery-green olive trees. The terraced hillsides and fertile valleys have been farmed for generations. The gorgeous landscape of the West Bank is filled with rocky, rolling hills.

Distances in Israel are strikingly small, but the changes in weather and landscape can be drastic. In one hour, you can go from the cool, breezy mountains of Jerusalem to the flat, humid seaside town of Tel Aviv. The coastal plain of the north and its bordering rich farmland, with chalk and sandstone cliffs, is home to deepwater ports.

A number of mountain ranges run from north to south through the landscape. In the perpetually green north, the volcanic eruption-created basalt Golan Heights tower over the Hula Valley. In the Galilee, where some elevations go as high as 4,000 feet above sea level, the hills are mostly dolomite and soft limestone.

Between Israel and the West Bank in the north is the Jezreel Valley, another fertile valley that is heavily cultivated.

Previous: people walking to the mosque at the Temple Mount; David and Goliath sculpture at the Tower of David Museum citadel.

Along the eastern side of Israel, part of the Syrian-African Rift that split the crust of the earth millions of years ago, are the Jordan Valley and the Arava. The land ranges from semiarid in the south to fertile in the north.

The south of Israel is home to the Negev Desert, and although it accounts for about half of the country's landmass, it is the least inhabited. The extremely arid south is made up of low sandstone hills and plains with a huge number of canyons amid the sandstone landscape that are prone to flash flooding in the winter. Campaigns to make the desert green with tree plantings have gained in popularity and practice, but the region is still largely desert.

A bit farther south, the Negev is characterized by barren stone peaks and plateaus littered with rocks. Here you will find three erosive craters that are so huge that they are tourist attractions. The largest, Ramon Crater, is about 5 miles across at its widest, about 24 miles long, and about 1,600 feet deep.

At the very south of Israel is Eilat and the Red Sea, where gray and red granite and sandstone form the base of the landscape.

SEAS AND RIVERS

One of the most significant bodies of water in the region is the Sea of Galilee. At 695 feet below sea level and between the hills of the Galilee and the Golan Heights, it is the most important source of water in Israel and home to several significant historic and religious sites.

The Sea of Galilee feeds the Jordan River and has a circumference of only about 30 miles. On the southern shore in the town of Tiberias, an electronic meter displays the Sea's water level, a number of national interest. In early 2013, following weeks of heavy rain, the sea level was higher than it had been in several years and ended a seven-year drought. In 2016, the sea suffered one of its worst years on record, though, prompting the announcement of another drought.

Coming from the southern mouth of the Sea of Galilee, the Jordan

the Sea of Galilee

River runs for about 186 miles, descending 2,300 feet from north to south through the Syrian-African Rift that split the crust of the earth millions of years ago. The river is fed by tributaries from Mount Hermon and empties into the Dead Sea, the lowest point on Earth. The Jordan Valley ranges from fertile in the north to semiarid in the south.

The Dead Sea sits at 1,300 feet below sea level on the southern end of the Jordan Valley. Its waters have the highest level of salinity and density of any body of water in the world, and are famed for their rich mineral deposits (and mud), which include table and industrial salt, bromine, magnesium, and potash.

Since 1960, the water level of the Dead Sea has dropped by more than 35 feet, partially caused by massive water diversion projects conducted by Israel and Jordan. The water diversion projects have reduced the amount of incoming water to the Dead Sea by 75 percent. In 2015, so many sinkholes had appeared in the land and sea from the lack of water that some public beaches and at least one hotel were closed for safety. Sinkholes continue to be a danger in the area.

South of the Dead Sea, which has separated into an upper section and a lower section over time, is the Arava, also part of the Syrian-African Rift and Israel's savanna region. The Arava continues to Israel's Red Sea outlet: the Gulf of Eilat, a subtropical region and home to some of the most remarkable coral reefs and unusual marinelife in the world.

CLIMATE

The climate in Israel and the West Bank vary widely from temperate to tropical to alpine. There are two distinct seasons, though two additional very brief transitions are often evident in between those.

Between November to May is the rainy season, or winter. Though it does not rain constantly, rainfall and lower temperatures (about 31°F at the lowest in some areas) do predominate.

From June through October, there is little to no rainfall, and the temperature rises steadily to a daily low of 66°F in some areas before starting its decline in late September. The average high throughout the country during the dry season ranges 84-104°F. The months of July and August are the most brutally punishing in terms of heat.

The variance in climate is marked by mild coastal winters, cooler summers in elevated regions (such as Jerusalem), and almost year-round semi-desert conditions in the Negev.

ENVIRONMENTAL ISSUES
Drought and Flash Floods

One of the major environmental issues in the region is drought. The mean annual rainfall is a mere 8 inches in the south and about 28 inches in the north.

In the winter months, the rainfall that does come can sometimes cause flash floods, particularly in the south with its canyons of bone-dry rock.

On occasion, a person or an animal will get swept away by one of these flash floods that seem to come out of nowhere, though that is rare.

Heat Waves

The punishing heat of the summer months (particularly during July and August) becomes more pronounced during a prolonged heat wave when the temperature can reach 95-105°F and higher, even in typically temperate Jerusalem. The greatest risk during heat waves to humans is suffering from dehydration or heatstroke, of which some of the symptoms are dizziness, nausea, confusion, blurred vision, and vomiting. Left untreated, dehydration and heatstroke can lead to complications that can cause death. It is imperative to drink plenty of water while in the region and to protect yourself from the sun, even when there is no heat wave.

Sandstorms

On rare occasion the air can be filled with a very fine, yellow dust, typically at the end of a heat wave. It is not exactly a sandstorm, but it turns the air yellow and leaves a layer of dust on everything, including your skin. Sand in the air at the end of a heat wave typically indicates that the heat wave is about to break and is usually followed by a brief rainfall that turns things a bit muddy.

History

The histories of the regions of Israel and the West Bank are long, winding, complex, and interconnected. In modern times, differing claims and versions of historical events are very much part of conversations and actions taken related to the land and political stances on important issues. In other words, the history of this region is very much alive and well and plays an active role in dictating the future.

ANCIENT CIVILIZATION

Canaan is the area generally defined as Palestine in historical and biblical literature, and is known today as Israel and the West Bank (also called Judea and Samaria or Palestine). The names of Canaan and Canaanites for its inhabitants appear in Egyptian and Phoenician writings from approximately the 15th century BC and in the Old Testament of the Bible. The earliest human inhabitants of coastal Canaan go back to Paleolithic and Mesolithic times. Evidence of human settlements has been found in Jericho dating back to 8000 BC.

Israelites conquered Palestine around the late 2nd century BC or earlier, but there were others before them. The Egyptians, the Hyksos, and the Hurrians also invaded. During the Late Bronze Age, about 1550-1200 BC, the Egyptians were the main dominating power in the region, despite challenges from the Hittites and the Hapiru, who some believe were the original Hebrews.

Most archaeological excavations of the area have been conducted since the 20th century, and the most significant literary texts on regional history are the Old Testament, the Ras Shamra texts, and the Amarna Letters, dispatches from the 14th century BC from Palestinian and Syrian governors to their Egyptian rulers.

The history and culture of the region has been influenced by a number of cultures, including Egyptian, Mycenaean, Cretan, Hurrian, Byzantine, Mesopotamian, Greek, Roman, and British. It is believed that the Canaanites were the first people to have used an alphabet, based on an archaeological discovery of a language that is widely recognized as a parent language to the Greek and Latin alphabets.

Around the time of the Early Iron Age, approximately 1250 BC, the Israelites came into Canaan after their exodus from Egypt and 40 years of wandering in the desert. In the next century, the Philistines invaded and established a strong hold over the region through a series of city-states, but it was broken under King David's leadership. King David also managed to capture Jerusalem from the Canaanites. The 10th century marked the beginning of the land being known as Israel.

Around the time of King David (about 1000-960 BC), the various tribes of Israel were consolidated into a united kingdom. King David made the Canaanite city of Jerusalem his capital and according to tradition, moved the Ark of the Covenant there, which was believed to contain the living presence of God. Around the time of 960-920 BC, David's son, Solomon, carried out the wish of his deceased father to build a great temple to house the Ark. The period of Solomon's rule is associated with the peak of Israelite grandeur; King Solomon oversaw the building of the First Temple, which was later destroyed. He also managed to forge treaties with neighboring kingdoms, including Egypt and Sheba, and create other important building projects in addition to the Temple.

The Kingdom of Israel was guided by strong, spiritual, monotheistic beliefs in one all-powerful God (Yahweh), the Lord Creator of the Universe. That belief was often used by rulers to help unify the kingdom and its people.

Around 920 BC, Solomon died, and the kingdom splintered into north and south halves. Israel was in the north with its capital Samaria, and the Kingdom of Judah was in the south with its capital Jerusalem. A period of frequent instability and lack of unity between the north and south followed, and by 721 BC, the Neo-Assyrian Empire became the new ruling force, expelling people to make room for its own settlements. In 587 BC, Jerusalem was sacked by the Babylonian king Nebuchadnezzar II. The Temple was destroyed, and the ruling class and skilled craftsmen were deported to Babylon.

The deportation by the Neo-Assyrians and Babylonians of the people of the Kingdom of Israel was the end of the existence of the nation of Israel until the modern state's creation in 1948. It also marked the beginning of the Jewish Diaspora and the start of the development of a religious framework in Judaism outside of the land of Israel. Connections between the ancient state and the modern state, including the name, remain an oft-debated and emotionally charged issue.

EARLY HISTORY

After the destruction of the First Temple, between 538-142 BC, there were several waves of tens of thousands of Jews who were allowed to return to Israel. They had varying degrees of self-rule over a period of about four centuries under Persian and Hellenistic authority.

Construction of a Second Temple on the site of the first one began in 521 BC and was finished in 516, during a period when Jerusalem's city walls were refortified.

Around 37 BC, Herod the Great was appointed king of Judea by the Romans and he launched a massive construction campaign, the evidence of which can be seen today in Caesarea, Masada, Jerusalem, and Herodium. Herod remodeled and renewed the Temple to a state of grandeur, but his efforts to appease the subjects to his rule failed to win their loyalty.

After a relatively brief period rule by the Hasmonean dynasty of Seleucids, the Romans came into power around 40 BC, and Israel became a Roman province. It was not long after this that Jesus appeared in Jerusalem and other areas in what is now Israel and the West Bank. According to tradition, he performed many miracles in Jerusalem, spread his teachings, and while standing atop the Mount of Olives, wept over the coming destruction of the holy city. Jerusalem is also where Jesus was crucified, buried, and said to have risen from the dead.

ancient Roman ruins at Caesarea

By AD 66, ongoing violence and anger against Roman rule and oppression had erupted into full-scale revolt. By AD 70, Jerusalem, including the Second Temple, had been razed to the ground by the Romans. The account by the well-known contemporary historian Josephus Flavius tells that hundreds of thousands of Jews died in the siege on Jerusalem and throughout Israel, including in the siege on the last stand of Jewish revolutionaries at Masada. Thousands more were sold into slavery.

Several hundred years later after generations of Roman rule and the declaration of Christianity as the official religion of the Roman kingdom around AD 325, Helena, mother of Constantine the Great, came to the Holy Land to begin construction of some of the world's first churches.

Under Helena's supervision, construction commenced on the Church of the Nativity (where Jesus is said to have been born), the Chapel of the Apostles on the Mount of Olives (where Jesus is said to have ascended to heaven), the Church of the Holy Sepulchre (where Jesus is said to have been crucified, buried, and resurrected), and another structure near Hebron.

During the 7th century, Jerusalem was the object of military conquest multiple times. It was sacked and claimed first by the Persians, then taken back by the Byzantines, and finally by the Islamic Empire. Around 690, under the rule of the Islamic Empire, the Dome of the Rock was built on the Temple Mount at the site of the First and Second Temples. According to Islamic tradition, the site is where Prophet Muhammad ascended to heaven. The region would remain under Islamic rule until about 1099.

Between the 8th and 9th centuries, the seventh of a series of historically massive and powerful earthquakes struck the region, destroying Tiberias, Beit She'an, Hippos, and Pella.

Between 1099 and 1291, the Crusaders and their multiple campaigns to reclaim the Holy Land dominated the region, until the ancient city of Akko fell to the Egyptians and the Crusader kingdom of Jerusalem was ended. The land was under Mamluk rule until 1516 when the Ottomans took over and ruled until 1917.

MODERN HISTORY

Near the end of the 400 years of Ottoman rule, in 1860 the first neighborhood was built outside the Old City walls of Jerusalem, and the First Aliya, a large-scale immigration of Jews, came to Israel. The Second Aliya came between 1904 and 1914. Both groups were mainly from Russia and Poland. By 1909, the first modern, all-Jewish city of Tel Aviv had been founded, and by 1917, British conquest had seized power from the Ottomans with the promise of a "Jewish national home in Palestine" by Foreign Minister Balfour.

The years between 1918 and 1948 were marked by British rule, and more groups of Aliya from Europe. In 1922, the British granted the Mandate for Palestine, with 75 percent of the area going to Transjordan (modern-day Jordan) and 25 percent designated for Jews. In this period, major universities were established in Haifa (Technion) and Jerusalem (Hebrew University).

During the British Mandate prior to World War II, there were several instances of significant violence and fighting between Arabs, who had been living in the region for centuries, and Jews. By 1947, the United Nations proposed the establishment of both Arab and Jewish states in the land of Israel.

MODERN WARS

Achieving the seemingly elusive peace between Arabs and Jews in the region has been an incredibly long and drawn-out process that started before Israel was ever officially a state. In May 1948, the British Mandate ended and the State of Israel was established.

The day after the state was formally declared, five Arab countries invaded Israel, marking the beginning of the War of Independence which lasted until 1949, when armistice agreements were signed with Egypt, Jordan, Syria, and Lebanon. Jerusalem was divided into east and west with East Jerusalem under Jordanian rule and West Jerusalem under Israeli rule. In 1948-1952, there were massive waves of immigration from European and Arab countries.

In 1967, the Six-Day War reunited Jerusalem's east and west sides of the city, though the east side is now technically part of the West Bank. The Six-Day War was followed by the Egyptian War of Attrition (1968-1970) and the Yom Kippur War (1973). Following the Camp David Accords, the Israel-Egypt Peace Treaty was signed, normalizing relations between the two countries.

After peace with Egypt and Jordan, internal domestic violence erupted in 1987 in Israel-administered areas with the First Intifada, followed by the Gulf War (1991). On the verge of a domestic peace agreement in 1995, then Prime Minister Yitzhak Rabin was assassinated in Tel Aviv. By 2000, the Second Intifada erupted, followed by years of violent internal regional instability.

In 2005, the highly controversial Gaza Disengagement Plan was carried out under the leadership of Prime Minister Ariel Sharon (who had a stroke and went into a coma almost immediately afterward), whereby Israel unilaterally withdrew all Jewish settlements in Gaza. Subsequently falling under the rule of the terrorist organization Hamas, Gaza has become a hotbed of violence and the center of destruction when fighting breaks out between Hamas and Israel.

BACKGROUND
HISTORY

GOVERNMENT

There are two governments in the region, one for Israel and one for the West Bank: the government of the State of Israel and the Palestinian Authority. If and when there is an agreement made about a two-state solution for the region, it will be made between these two bodies. However, the major power in the region, politically, economically, legally, and militarily, is Israel.

Symbolism

The flag of the State of Israel is designed based on the Jewish prayer shawl with the blue star of David in the center. Israel's official emblem is a menorah flanked by olive branches that represent Israel's desire for peace. The national anthem, *Hatikvah,* was penned by Jewish poet Naphtali Herz Imber in 1878, and the words express the hope of the Jewish people to live as a free and sovereign people in the land of Israel.

The flag used to represent the State of Palestine is a tricolor flag with three equal horizontal stripes of black, white, and green, with a sideways triangle of red on the left. It is based on a variety of different flags, including the one used during the 1916 Arab revolt.

Israeli Government Organization

The Israeli government is a parliamentary democracy, with free elections, a prime minister, and a president. The system is based on the concept of a division of powers between the legislative, executive, and judicial branches.

POLITICAL PARTIES AND ELECTIONS

Israel's unicameral parliament is called the Knesset, and functions in plenary sessions through 15 standing committees and 120 members. The Knesset generally runs for terms of four years, and its makeup is determined after general elections. Both Hebrew and Arabic are officially recognized languages of the Knesset, though debates on issues are conducted in Hebrew with simultaneous translation if a member wishes to speak Arabic.

The party with the most power in the Knesset following the 2015 elections is Likud, the party of Prime Minister Benjamin "Bibi" Netanyahu.

Israeli citizens are eligible to vote from age 18, and they vote for a political party to represent them in the Knesset, not for individuals. There are a wide range of political parties that run for seats in the Knesset representing a broad range of beliefs and positions on the issues.

Election Day in Israel is a national holiday, and if a voter is outside of their polling district, free transportation is provided to them. Polling stations are provided for military personnel, prisoners, hospital patients, merchant sailors, and Israelis on official work abroad.

Israel's political situation is characterized largely by a range of staunch advocates and lukewarm alliances. Immediately in Israel's neighborhood, Egypt and Jordan are border countries that have generally good relations with Israel. Relations with Turkey blow hot and cold, and Israel is not on good terms with Syria, Lebanon, or Iran.

The positions of western countries vary, but the United States is Israel's single greatest ally in the world. Other countries like Australia and Canada are basically supportive, but there is a great deal of political activism over the plight of Palestinians that originates in the west. The United Kingdom is on good terms with Israel, but its public discourse regularly challenges Israel's settlement policies in the West Bank and its human rights record vis-à-vis Arab residents of the West Bank and Israel.

JUDICIAL AND PENAL SYSTEMS

Israel's judiciary system is independent. Judges are appointed by the president after being recommended by a committee of Supreme Court judges, public figures, and members of the bar. Judicial appointments are permanent until mandatory retirement at age 70.

There are several types of courts, including special courts (such as traffic, labor, juvenile), religious courts, magistrates' court, district court, and the Supreme Court.

ISRAELI MILITARY

The Israeli Defense Force (IDF) has been tested in battle through several generations since the establishment of the State of Israel in 1948, and has fought in six major wars and numerous smaller ones. The highest-level public officials and politicians were often individuals who distinguished themselves during military service and in war.

Service in the IDF is compulsory for all eligible men and women at the age of 18. The male term of service is three years, while women serve for two years, and deferments can be made for students or new immigrants. Reserve duty obligations continue for men until age 51, and every soldier serves in a reserve unit that they are called to work for at least once a year. Ultraorthodox members of society are exempt from military service.

Palestinian Authority Government Organization

The Palestinian National Authority, also called the Palestinian Authority (PA), was established as an interim self-governing authority following the Oslo accords in 2003. The PA governs parts of the West Bank. It used to also govern Gaza, which is now under the control of Hamas.

The PA embodies many of the characteristics of a state, including a legislative and executive body, and a semi-independent judiciary.

Leadership includes a president, cabinet, and a prime minister.

The Palestinian Authority military patrols certain areas of the West Bank, including some parts of Bethlehem, Hebron, Ramallah, and some checkpoints. They are largely a peacekeeping force.

ECONOMY

The Israeli economy was started virtually from scratch almost 70 years ago (officially) and has weathered crises and deprivation of various kinds. The modern free-market economy is bolstered by R&D, high-tech industries, nanotechnology, solar energy, irrigation innovation, agriculture, and a thriving start-up scene admired internationally.

Exports and Imports

In the past 30 years, significant free trade agreements have been made with the United States, the European Union, and a number of countries in Latin America. Israel's export of goods and services is about $80 billion annually.

Israel has struggled to balance its hefty trade deficit, which has been the price for its rapid economic growth. The somewhat limited domestic market and small economy mean that Israel must rely on expansion of exports, particularly industrial exports.

Most imports, about 85 percent, are production inputs and fuel, largely from Europe, followed by the Americas, then Asia, and other countries. Most exports of goods go to the United States, Europe, and Asia. Excluding the export of diamonds, Israel's exports to the United States exceed its imports, but its overall imports exceed its exports.

Almost two-thirds of Israel's annual trade deficits have been covered through unilateral transfers, including foreign pensions, money brought in by immigrants, and hefty donations from overseas Jewish fundraising organizations that have gone straight into the coffers of health, education, and social service organizations and institutions. Grants from generous foreign governments, particularly the United States, have also bolstered the economy.

Agriculture

Scarce natural resources, particularly water and arable land, define Israel's production system in its agricultural sector. Aggressive innovation and ongoing cooperation between researchers, farmers, and agricultural industries drive the growth in agricultural production. The development and application of new methods across the board have fostered a sophisticated modern agricultural industry in a country where more than half of the land is desert.

The dogged innovation of the Israeli agricultural industry and its close cooperation with the R&D world have fostered a marketable international agribusiness export sector with agro-technology solutions. Particularly valuable to the outside and developing world have been innovations in regard to water.

The wide variety of creative solutions developed in response to extremely limited water resources include desalinization plants and drip agriculture.

Most of the country's food and flowers are produced domestically and supplemented by imports that mainly include grain, oilseeds, meat, coffee, cocoa, and sugar. Israel exports heavily to Europe during the winter, sending fruits, vegetables, and flowers.

Industry

Israel has overcome the small size of its country and its lack of raw materials and natural resources by focusing on its highly qualified workforce, R&D centers, and scientific institutes. The country's modern industry is centered around the manufacturing of products with added value. Today, over a quarter of the industrial workforce works in high-tech manufacturing.

Much of Israel's modern manufacturing base was developed straight out of 19th-century workshops that produced farming implements and processed agricultural products. When entrepreneurs and engineers with years of experience immigrated to Israel in the 1930s, they were followed by an increased demand for industrial products during World War II.

Most of the industrial output from Israel centered around traditional products like food processing, furniture, chemicals, plastics, and other items, until the 1970s. This output was followed by a period marked by arms embargoes, which forced industrialization to focus on developing and manufacturing arms for self-defense. Massive investment in the arms industry and aviation gave life to new technologies that would later be the foundation of Israel's high-tech industries. These include medical devices, telecommunications, computer software and hardware, and more.

Two waves of human resources in the 1980s and 1990s bolstered the fledgling high-tech industries: first, the return of Israelis who had been working in Silicon Valley to open development centers for multinationals including Intel, Microsoft, and IBM; second, the huge wave of technicians, scientists, medical workers, and engineers who fled the former Soviet Union in the 1990s after its fall.

Another ace in the hole in Israel's industrial sector is the diamond industry. The country's reputation as a high-quality source for diamond manufacturing and trading has made it a leader in the industry. Tel Aviv's famed diamond district is just one of the ways that the country showcases its cutting-edge technologies, competitive prices, and high yield of polished diamonds from the rough. The Israel Diamond Exchange is the largest diamond trading floor in the world, and diamond exports are in the neighborhood of about $10 billion a year. Most imports are sent to the United States, Hong Kong, Belgium, and Switzerland.

Entrepreneurship and Invention

Israel has earned a reputation for being a hotbed of entrepreneurship, innovation, and invention, bolstered in part by the publication of a book called *Start-up Nation: The Story of Israel's Economic Miracle*, which details the numerous ways in which the country has repeatedly innovated and invented its way into the 21st century.

The premise of the book is based on the fact that despite being a young country with a population of just over 8.4 million and surrounded by enemies, Israel is home to more start-up companies than Japan, China, India, Korea, Canada and the United Kingdom combined.

Distribution of Wealth

In 2011, massive, long-term public protests over Israel's distribution of wealth broke out throughout the country, centered mostly in Tel Aviv. The protests evolved into weeks-long encampments, mostly of young people, who demanded a more equitable distribution of economic wealth and a more equitable distribution of economic burden in their society.

Between 2005 and 2007, Israel had a millionaire boom, producing more millionaires per capita than any country in the world. The current estimated net worth of Israel's 500 richest people is in the neighborhood of US$140 billion (the country's GDP is about US$306 billion).

One of the most serious issues in the debate about the distribution of wealth stems from the perceived affordability of housing among the middle and lower class. The purchase of second homes in Jerusalem and Tel Aviv by wealthy foreigners is seen as having a major impact on housing prices. In the past eight years, housing prices in some neighborhoods in Israel have risen by 25 percent. Settlements and apartment prices in the West Bank, on the other hand, remain extremely affordable.

Tourism

Israel's most frequently visited cities, Jerusalem and Tel Aviv, continue to work hard to become international tourist destinations. With the gradual stabilizing of the internal security of Israel has come a stabilized tourism base. Since 2010, the average number of visitors to the country has been

a group of visitors in Jerusalem

about three million people per year. Most visitors come from Europe, and about a quarter are from the United States. Since 2015, the numbers of tourists to some cities has dropped by as much as 40 percent, in large part due to spates of violence and conflict.

An average of about 30 percent of people visit Israel on a pilgrimage, while others come for leisure, to visit family, or on business. The vast majority of all tourists (about 80 percent), no matter why they are visiting the country, include Jerusalem as a destination. About 65 percent include Tel Aviv as a destination, about 45 percent go to the Dead Sea, and about 20 percent go to Tiberias and the Sea of Galilee.

People and Culture

DEMOGRAPHY

When the State of Israel was established, the country's population was about 806,000. Today it is more than 8.4 million. About 75 percent of residents are Jewish, over 20 percent are Arab, and all other groups make up just over 4 percent of the population. Over 70 percent of the total Jewish population was born in Israel; a native-born Jewish Israeli is known as a *sabra*.

Israel has 14 cities with over 100,000 residents; the 6 cities of Jerusalem, Tel Aviv-Yafo, Haifa, Rishon LeTsiyon, Petah Tikva, and Ashdod all have over 200,000 residents.

Israel has had periods of massive, concentrated immigration tied to world events. In 1990 alone, after the fall of the Soviet Union, more than 199,000 immigrants came to Israel, and another 176,000 in 1991. In the past few years, however, there has been an average of 16,500 immigrants to the country per year.

Israel suffers severely on the international stage from problems related to religious and ethnic tensions between the Jewish majority and Arab minority, which impacts its ability to attract a larger number of tourists and immigrants. Though daily life in major cities such as Tel Aviv, Jerusalem, and elsewhere is largely peaceful and various ethnicities and religions peacefully coexist, violence does erupt on a fairly regular basis. With the rule of neighboring Gaza in the hands of Hamas, the greatest domestic threat comes from attacks that originate in Gaza, such as rocket attacks. In recent years, isolated acts of violence carried out by individuals have also been on the rise, particularly beginning in 2015.

The West Bank, with its complex and multilayered governance and distribution of security between the Palestinian Authority and Israel, is also sometimes the source of religious and ethnic tension, protests, and violence.

Jews

As an ethnic group, Jews constitute about 75 percent of the population of

Israel. Of those, about 72 percent are Israel-born and about 19 percent are European or American-born. About 9 percent were born in Africa and Asia.

Arabs

The Arab population of Israel stands at about 23 percent and includes those who are Muslim, Christian, and Jewish. Bedouin and Druze peoples fall under the category of the Arab population.

RELIGION

Though Israel is officially a Jewish state, for all intents and purposes residents of Israel enjoy religious freedom to practice whatever faith they choose.

Those who are registered with the government as practicing Judaism comprise about 58 percent of the population, non-Arab Christians are about 2 percent, and those not classified by religion are almost 5 percent. Of Israel's Arab population, 84 percent (about 20 percent of the population) are practicing Muslims, and almost 8 percent are Arab Christians. Another 9 percent are Druze.

Judaism

More than 58 percent of the people of Israel identify themselves as practicing the religion of Judaism, an ancient monotheistic faith with varying degrees of orthodoxy. The degree of orthodoxy of the Diaspora of people who practice Judaism around the world varies. The same is true in Israel, with pockets of people practicing orthodox, ultraorthodox, and reform Judaism, to name a few.

Particularly in Jerusalem but also throughout Israel and the West Bank, religious individuals can be somewhat identified by their dress. The men wear long, black coats and large black hats, and the women dress in long

reading the Torah in Jerusalem

skirts and dresses with their arms and legs covered, and their heads covered with a hat, scarf, or wig.

On the day of worship on Friday, religious services are performed in synagogues. The more religious synagogues separate men and women into different worship areas. The holiest site in the holiest city to Jews is the Western Wall in Jerusalem (also known as the Kotel). It is the last remaining piece of the outer wall of the courtyard of the great temple that was twice built and destroyed on that spot in history.

Christianity

The Christian community in Israel, which is about 2 percent of the population, represents a wide variety of different sects from all over the world. There are Greek Orthodox, Russian Orthodox, Catholic, and others. Though they are only a small part of the population overall in the country, the Roman Catholic Church owns a large portion of land in Jerusalem.

Islam

About 20 percent of Israel's population practices the religion of Islam; they are known as Muslims. The Islamic religion, in general, is fairly strict and generally forbids drinking alcohol. Friday is the day of prayer for Muslims, which makes it a difficult day to visit the Old City, as Al Aqsa Mosque (the third holiest site in Islam) becomes very crowded.

Religious services are performed in mosques, which can often be distinguished by the nearby minaret (tower) from which the call to prayer is broadcast five times a day. In terms of dress, Muslim women (especially in more conservative areas like Nablus in the West Bank) dress in a very covered-up manner with headscarves, long sleeves, and covered legs. In some cases women's faces and hands are also covered.

Al Aqsa Mosque is the third holiest site in Islam.

Israel has two official languages: Hebrew and Arabic. But English is a compulsory second language taught throughout much of the secondary level education system, so the majority of Hebrew speakers and many Arabic speakers also speak and understand English at least at a conversational level.

Almost all signs, menus, transportation tables, and tourist information are written in English.

THE ARTS

The arts in Israel are a well-developed and robust part of society. In addition to the many skills and traditions that generations of immigrants have brought with them from their original countries, the indigenous arts, crafts, and culture play a significant role.

Literature

Israel's literary culture is dominated by Hebrew-speaking authors, but in recent years the Arabic-speaking community has also made significant breakthroughs and contributions.

An ongoing issue in Israel's literary community is the slow death that independent booksellers are suffering due to the existence of a couple of major national chains. These chains are often accused of selling books at much less than their value, angering both authors and independent booksellers, who cannot compete with the prices. In recent years, many independent booksellers have been forced into closing.

Despite the challenges to independent sellers, you can still find a variety of different types of bookstores in major cities that sell material in various languages including Hebrew, Arabic, French, and English. Major periodicals in English, Arabic, French, and sometimes Russian are also sold at national chain stores and smaller shops.

Jerusalem hosts a renowned international literature conference every year, but it is sometimes overshadowed by authors who choose to publicly boycott attending on the grounds of concerns over Israel's presence in the West Bank and its position on issues related to the Arab population. The largest Arab city of Ramallah also hosts an annual Literary Festival.

Visual Arts

The thriving visual arts scene in Israel is supported by the large number of museums, from the Israel Museum in Jerusalem to the Tel Aviv Museum of Art, to scores of venues of all sizes. Modern visual art in Israel shows international influences and the meeting of East and West, and reflects the influences of the land, traditions, and cultures.

Visual artists in Israel are engaged in a wide range of disciplines, including painting, photography, and sculpture. Part of what makes Israeli visual art unique is its emphasis and reflections on the local landscape, domestic social issues, and politics.

The thriving dance scene in Israel has developed mainly in the Jewish folk dance genre and artistic dance centered around stage productions. The major influence of European dance began in the 1920s, and has developed to a highly professional level through a number of companies and ensembles. Dance in Israel is influenced by the region's various social, cultural, and religious backgrounds.

There are currently over a dozen major professional dance companies in Israel, mostly in Tel Aviv, that perform domestically and internationally. There are also dance groups based in Ramallah.

The annual Israel Festival is the country's major multidisciplinary arts festival, held over a period of a few weeks in Jerusalem.

The music scene in Israel is just as vibrant as other places in the world, if not more. The country's offerings start with the world-class classical music of the Israeli Philharmonic Orchestra and the New Israeli Opera. The country's music scene has been enhanced by waves of European immigrants who brought along skills and influences from the best traditions in the world. The variations of music genres range from Arabic and Hebrew pop to Middle Eastern jazz, rock, and mainstream American music.

Essentials

Transportation

GETTING THERE

There are a variety of ways to get to this region, though most visitors arrive by air through the international airport in Tel Aviv.

Air

Tel Aviv's **Ben Gurion International Airport** (tel. 03/975-2386, www.iaa.gov.il) is a massive, modern airport with flights to and from almost everywhere in the world. It is about a 15-minute drive from Tel Aviv and about one hour from Jerusalem. Once at the airport, you can easily get to your destination by hotel shuttle, train, taxi, *sherut* (share taxi), or bus.

During the Jewish Sabbath—late Friday afternoon until Saturday night—things slow down considerably. The airport is still open, but certain airlines might not operate (such as Israel's El Al) and public transportation to and from the airport doesn't operate. Yom Kippur, when almost nobody drives and all public transportation shuts down, would present problems.

Boat

Some people traveling by boat end up visiting Israel while on their way somewhere else, such as cruise ship passengers who stay for 1-2 days and longer, and some are ferry passengers who are traveling with cars. Both types of passengers go through the international **Port of Haifa** (www.haifaport.co.il). The port includes a large terminal with a wide variety of passenger facilities, including a waiting area, a duty-free shop, a souvenir shop, a cafeteria, a VAT (Value Added Tax) reimbursement counter and currency exchange, a Ministry of Interior services office, and other travel-related services.

Typical customs and immigrations procedures apply for passengers who want to exit the port and enter Israel. There is long- and short-term parking next to the passenger terminal. People on foot can walk about 10 minutes to the port's exit and take a taxicab to wherever they are going in Haifa.

Land

From **Jordan** (www.visitjordan.com) there are three land border crossings into Israel from the north, center, and south. The central and southern border crossings are the most convenient and frequently used, while the northernmost crossing is isolated from major cities and attractions.

The **Wadi Araba Crossing/South Border** (6:30am-8pm Sun.-Thurs., 8am-8pm Fri.-Sat.) connects the resort towns of Eilat in Israel and Aqaba in Jordan. Visas are issued on the spot at the Eilat crossing, and you don't need to provide photographs.

The **Allenby/King Hussein Bridge** is in the southern Jordan Valley (8am-8pm for entering Jordan, 8am-2pm for leaving Jordan Sun.-Thurs., 8am-1pm Fri.-Sat.). Private cars and tour buses are not allowed to cross, so you have to change vehicles when crossing the border. If coming from Israel, pay for your visa in advance (about JD16) at the Jordanian embassy in Tel Aviv, and you will need two photographs. You will receive a visa within 24 hours.

Americans and Canadians coming from Jordan into Israel do not need to apply for a visa in advance. They will be issued a visa at the crossing. There will usually be an exit fee of JD10 when coming from Jordan into Israel. Always travel with a passport that is valid for at least six months beyond your dates of travel.

GETTING AROUND

It is fairly easy to get around Israel because of the excellent bus systems that exist nationally and within the large cities. The various train systems are less convenient because of their somewhat limited routes and slow pace, but they do offer a good option for transportation.

Train

The national train system, the **Israel Railways** (www.rail.co.il), is a fairly convenient way to get around many parts of Israel, particularly useful for north to south routes. Just be aware that the railway system is also plagued by ongoing issues that include labor strikes and problems with keeping to the timetable. Daily and multi-journey tickets are available, and kids under the age of five travel for free.

The station stops in Jerusalem are quite far off the beaten path, on the outskirts of town near the zoo and the Malha Mall. Just to get to and from

Ben Gurion International Airport in Tel Aviv

the Jerusalem train station to the city center, you will need to take a taxi, bus, or car.

If you go by train from the airport, you can be in Jerusalem in about 2.5 hours (the route from the airport to Jerusalem is abnormally long). There are several train lines that leave every 20-30 minutes from the airport.

Train etiquette at crowded stops when passengers are boarding and disembarking is somewhat nonexistent. Basically, be prepared to shove your way on or off the train or risk getting stuck.

Bus

The main bus company that essentially comprises the national bus system of long-distance routes in Israel runs the green and white **Egged** (www. egged.co.il/Eng) buses. They can get you almost anywhere you want to go. Overall information about buses in Israel is online (http://bus.co.il).

You can pay cash for your bus ticket (about NIS7 within the city) while boarding the bus and do not need to wait at the ticket window if you are traveling from the central bus station. If you know you'll be making a return trip, buy your ticket on the bus and you will get a small discount. Central bus stations in major cities display route information in English and Hebrew on monitors in the station.

You can also buy a Rav Kav Card for 10 or 20 rides, also good for transfers, and each ride will be at a small discount.

Once you are on the bus, depending on where you are going, there are a few things to be aware of. First of all, the safety rules are fairly loose, and when seats are sold out on a long-distance bus, you can sit or stand in the aisle or the stairwell at the back of the bus. Eating and drinking are allowed, but if traveling with Jewish orthodox passengers (distinguishable by their black hats, black coats, beards, and white shirts), it is advisable to avoid sitting next to them.

The public transportation depot at the Tel Aviv airport is on the second floor near Gates 21 and 23. Buses go from there to the Egged station at nearby Airport City, and then you can transfer to regular Egged bus lines. The buses from Airport City to the airport are free. The Egged buses will get you to south Tel Aviv's Central Bus Station.

You can also go between Jerusalem's Central Bus Station and the airport by Egged bus. It takes about one hour in normal traffic. Try to avoid making the trip on a Friday afternoon, as traffic will typically be the worst at that time.

In Jerusalem, the bus system is extremely convenient, and the buses are frequent. There is a discounted public transportation ticket for tourists for public buses, operated by Egged. There is also a double-decker city tour bus that you can hop on and off all day long at major sights after buying a 24- or 48-hour ticket. The one-stop shop for Jerusalem transportation information, including the buses, is **Jerusalem Transportation** (www.jet. gov.il). A one-way ticket is about NIS7 and cannot be used for transfers.

At the time of publication the only city in the entire country of Israel with buses that operate on the weekend (with partial service) is Haifa. The closest thing to public transportation that is available in other cities on the weekend is the *sherut* (share taxis), which are more expensive and less convenient.

Light-Rail

Jerusalem's **light-rail** (tel. 073/210-0601 or *3686 from any local phone, www.citypass.co.il, 5:30am-midnight Sun.-Thurs., 5:30am-3pm Fri. and holiday eves, 7pm-midnight Sat., NIS5.9 for a single ride, or multi-ride on Rav Kav Card) offers a fast and convenient way to get around certain parts of the city.

Tourists get a discounted public transportation ticket, but there is not an extensive network of stops throughout the city. All tickets are valid for continued use for 90 minutes from the time they were purchased.

The route of Jerusalem's light-rail is fairly limited, but there are plans to expand it. It is roughly along the old border between East and West Jerusalem, and it is convenient if you want to get somewhere in East Jerusalem. It has stops next to the *shuk,* City Center, Mount Herzl, and Yad Vashem.

Taxi and Share Taxi

Throughout Israel, **taxicabs** are everywhere, but most cost 25 percent more on weekends and between 9pm-5am. One good option if you want to order a cab to come and pick you up (which will cost about NIS5 extra) is to ask any hotel front desk for the name of a taxi company. A company that operates nationally and is recommended by the Municipality of Jerusalem is **Rehavia Taxi** (Taxi Stand at 3 Agron St. in Jerusalem, tel. 02/625-4444 or 02/622-2444).

Sherut (**share taxis**) are an option in most parts of the country, and especially for travel between Jerusalem and Tel Aviv. On the weekend, they are your best (and almost only) option. A *sherut* from Jerusalem to Tel Aviv is about NIS35 or less, and leaves from the base of Tolerance Square seven days a week. The *sherut* from Tel Aviv leaves from the Central Bus Station (106 Levinski St.), just east of Neve Tzedek and Florentin. Keep in mind that a *sherut* will only depart when all of the seats are full. Depending on how you time it, you might be waiting for 20-30 minutes for the taxi to fill up. While you're riding in the *sherut,* if you need to get out somewhere, it's perfectly acceptable to ask the driver to let you out as soon as possible; drivers stop upon request at the first chance they have to pull over.

Car

Americans in Israel are allowed to drive with their foreign license for up to one year after arriving in the country. There are quite a number of rental car companies that operate throughout Israel, the most prevalent of which are **Hertz** (19 King David St. in Jerusalem, tel. 02/623-1351, www.hertz.co.il) and **Budget** (23 King David St. in Jerusalem, tel. 03/935-0015),

ESSENTIALS
TRANSPORTATION

offering a wide variety of options; car rentals run about US$45 day after mandatory insurance is added. The largest domestic car rental company in Israel is **Eldan** (114 HaYarkon St. in Tel Aviv, tel. 03/527-1166, www. eldan.co.il); **Shlomo Sixt** (122 HaYarkon St. in Tel Aviv, tel. 03/524-4935, www.shlomo.co.il) is another good option. The central area for car rental offices in Jerusalem is on King David Street, just across from the King David Hotel, near Mamilla shopping center. In Tel Aviv, there is a stretch of car rental companies right on the promenade to the beach around 114 HaYarkon Street.

The parking system throughout Israel is uniform and has strict rules, but there are many unspoken exceptions, especially during the weekend when parking rules are suspended. For instance, you might see cars parked on the sidewalk, or facing the wrong direction when parked along the street.

Red and white stripes mean no parking; blue and white stripes signify paid parking by a street meter (a machine that sometimes only takes cash); and gray means free. Other paid parking in certain neighborhoods or small lots will have a yellow and black sign with hours of paid parking where you must buy a ticket and leave it on your car dash with the date stamp showing. Paid parking costs approximately NIS10 for 90 minutes.

If you are going to be driving on a daily basis for an extended period of time, Yellow gas stations sell an automatic pay in advance meter that you leave on the side of your vehicle. The meter costs NIS100 and you can pay for time on it as you go. If you have a smartphone, you may be able to install the Pango app which you can use to pay for parking.

Driving yourself is fairly straightforward, as 99 percent of the road signs are posted in English, Hebrew, and Arabic. Don't panic if you think you're on the right road but don't see signs, or see signs for something with a different spelling. It is not uncommon to have no signage to a certain place until the last minute, or for signage names to change in their spelling of the place. The best thing to do is stop and ask for directions. But be prepared to stop more than once because when people give directions in Israel they typically tell you to go to a certain point and then ask someone else.

If you drive into Jerusalem, take Highway 1 and just follow the signs. There are several exits to Jerusalem, some of which will take you far into the outskirts and hills of town. Try to keep as close to City Center as possible, as that is where most hotels are, and where you will have the best luck getting your bearings. Driving within the city of Jerusalem can be extremely complicated and confusing, so take your time, and if you think you are lost, don't hesitate to stop.

TIPS FOR DRIVING

The key to driving while you're in the Middle East is to stay calm and focused, which will help you navigate the tricky road rules. The general guidelines are to keep moving, don't be afraid to improvise (especially in Jerusalem), and don't be afraid to honk your horn. Particularly for Americans, honking can be taken as rude, but it is an important mode of communication in the Middle East, where the roads are often older and narrower.

Some roads were built during times when they were used by donkey carts and horses, so they aren't quite wide enough for cars. Other roads were built up the side of mountains as cities grew over hundreds of years and are extremely steep. Take your time and have a GPS with you wherever you go.

There is no right turn on red, and you probably won't get a ticket if you park on the side of the street facing the wrong way.

CHECKPOINTS

There are checkpoints posted in various locations between Israel and the West Bank, inside the West Bank at the edge of Israel-controlled territory, at the Tel Aviv airport, and at Gaza. Sometimes officers at a checkpoint will ask you to open your trunk, so know where that release is located and be ready to open it. If you are stopped at the airport, you might be asked a series of questions. Don't panic if you are questioned. It is typically related to whatever the current security situation is and not you personally. There are also security checkpoints going into most major buildings where you will need to open your bag for inspection.

GAS CONVERSION

The price of 95 octane gas in the government-regulated system at gas stations throughout Israel fluctuates, but is about NIS6 per liter. At full-service gas stations, it costs 0.18 more per liter. The price of gas is updated by the government once a month and published in all daily newspapers.

Hitchhiking

Hitchhiking for a ride in Israel and the West Bank is fairly common, but carries the same risks as hitchhiking anywhere else. The regional signal for someone seeking a ride is to point their index finger at the ground in

the checkpoint at Hebron in the West Bank

front of them. Especially on the weekend or on Friday afternoons, you will see more hitchhikers than usual.

If you are driving and see a soldier hitchhiking, understand that it is against military regulations for soldiers to hitchhike and they could face time in the brig if they are caught taking a ride.

Visas and Officialdom

Israeli bureaucracy is infamous, but getting into Israel from one of the many countries that they have a visa waiver program with is fairly easy.

VISAS AND PASSPORTS

If you have a passport that is valid for a minimum of six months after your date of exit from the country and you are coming from a visa waiver country, you do not have to arrange for a visa in advance to enter Israel. You will be automatically granted a three-month tourist visa upon entering Israel and there is no fee. The countries that have a visa waiver program with Israel include the United States, the United Kingdom, Australia, Canada, New Zealand, South Africa, and others.

If you plan to visit Arab countries (aside from Jordan) for the duration of your passport, ask for your visa stamp to Israel to be put on a separate piece of paper. It is not an uncommon request, as a passport with a stamp from Israel might make it very difficult or impossible to gain entry into many Arab countries.

ISRAELI EMBASSIES AND CONSULATES ABROAD

Israel maintains embassies and consulates all over the world. In the United States, there are Consulate General offices of Israel in New York, Atlanta, Boston, Houston, Chicago, Miami, Philadelphia, San Francisco, and Los Angeles, as well as the Israeli Embassy in Washington, D.C.

FOREIGN EMBASSIES AND CONSULATES IN ISRAEL

Though Jerusalem is Israel's capital city and the seat of its federal government, countries with diplomatic relations with Israel maintain their embassies in Tel Aviv. The reason for this is related to Jerusalem's complicated international legal status. If a foreign government established its embassy in Jerusalem (instead of the consulates there now), it might be seen as an indication of the recognition of Jerusalem as the capital city of Israel. It would also seriously complicate matters in the event that an independent Palestinian state was established. For that reason, embassies of foreign governments, including the United States, are located in Tel Aviv.

There are two locations for the Consulate of the United States in (main consulate at 18 Agron Rd., and consular services at 14 David Flusser St., tel. 02/630-4000 or 02/622-7230 for emergencies and during nonbusiness hours, http://jerusalem.usconsulate.gov). The consulate in East Jerusalem essentially straddles the east-west "border" of the city. Appointments are mandatory for all visits to the consulate.

The **U.S. Embassy in Tel Aviv** (71 HaYarkon St., tel. 03/519-7475 or 03/519-7575 for emergencies and during nonbusiness hours, http://israel. usembassy.gov) has a useful email alert system that tells American citizens of serious security threats and advises areas not to travel in during times of violence and unrest in the region. Before traveling to Israel, you can register with the consulate or embassy for alerts.

TAXES

The Israeli taxing system uses what they call a Value Added Tax (VAT) of more than 16 percent for the purchase of goods and services. VAT is included in the price of many items (such as restaurants). However, if you purchase a more expensive item as a gift or souvenir while in the country (minimum NIS400), ask for tax refund forms. You will be eligible to get the VAT back when going through customs. Note that non-Israeli citizens or people who are not residents of Israel are not required to pay VAT for items like hotels and car rentals.

CUSTOMS

The standard fare of items are prohibited for import by Israeli customs, including weapons and drugs. They also restrict the import of games of chance, pornographic material, plants and soil, and pets. You can bring up to US$200 worth of tax-free gifts into Israel, 250 grams of cigarettes, and one bottle of liquor. You can convert up to US$3,000 in cash at the airport when you leave.

Be particularly careful about buying any kind of antiquities or archaeological artifacts and then transporting them out of the country; you must have a certificate that identifies the object in question. If you buy from a licensed antiquities dealer, they will provide you with such a certificate.

MEDICAL REQUIREMENTS

Inoculations and vaccinations are not required for entry to Israel.

POLITICAL AFFILIATIONS AND AGENDAS

If you enter Israel with a specific intention or action that relates to a political agenda (particularly one that would be seen as against the state), you might be prevented from entering the country. This usually applies to large groups with a high profile, but you might be questioned by customs about the purpose of your trip to Israel.

POLICE

In some areas of Israel, there are **Tourist Police** (tel. 03/516-5382) who specifically work to serve tourists with any criminal matter (such as theft) or an emergency. You can also call the tourist police if you have an emergency.

Food

The food in Israel is basically a combination of a Mediterranean and Middle Eastern diet that emphasizes fruits, vegetables, whole grains, and non-processed foods, with a few common threads that can be found almost everywhere you go.

HUMMUS AND FALAFEL

Two of the most famous and favorite food dishes are hummus and falafel. Hummus is a sort of paste that is generally made from chickpeas, olive oil, and tahini. Hummus can be used as a dip on pita or on the side of your plate with main dishes, or as a sort of dressing on top of dishes like salad. It is also commonly used in shwarma sandwiches.

Falafel are deep-fried balls of mashed chickpeas that have been blended with onions and herbs. They can be bought from street vendors, in the *shuk,* and from small shops that specialize in falafel. Falafel is commonly served stuffed inside of a pita sandwich with lettuce, tomatoes, pickles, and tahini (a commonly served paste of sesame seeds and olive oil). It makes a filling and sometimes very cheap meal if you are not buying it in a tourist area.

SHWARMA

The many shops that sell shwarma are distinguishable by the large chunk of lamb meat cooking on a spit in a prominent location. The meat is cut

a typical breakfast in Israel

directly off of the spit and typically served in a pita sandwich. You can usually tell if a shwarma shop is good by how juicy the meat is. If customers are not coming to eat frequently, the meat might look a bit dried out.

BEDOUIN

Bedouin food, which can be found throughout the region, is traditionally cooked on an open fire and eaten with the hands. Common Bedouin meals include the more standard pita; the thin, crepe-like *shraak* pita that is cooked on a domed pan over a fire; and *taboon,* which is usually thicker and made from darker flour. Other typical Bedouin ingredients and dishes focus on lamb meat, rice, and yogurt.

DRUZE

Arab people of Syrian descent, the Druze are known for their delicious dishes that include many typical facets of Middle Eastern food, such as pita, hummus, vegetables, and lamb and chicken dishes. Druze stew, a delicious combination of meat, potatoes, and vegetables, is worth trying when you're in the region.

KOSHER AND NONKOSHER

Some areas of Israel have a multilayered system of following the religious dietary laws of being kosher. The level to which the restaurant follows kosher regulations determines the type of certificate it will display. Kosher certifications are always posted in public view and are often advertised on websites.

Particularly in Jerusalem, most restaurants are kosher, so they will either serve milk or meat, but not both. At a kosher restaurant that serves meat, for example, you will not be able to get a latte or ice cream for dessert. They might serve milk-substitute dishes, though, so it is always worth asking.

The production of kosher food is overseen by a rabbi who certifies the food as being kosher according to Jewish law. The level of supervision and adherence to religious dietary law determines the differing types of kosher certification. The three levels from least restricted to most restricted are kosher, glatt kosher, and mehadrin kosher.

Some hotels cater to religious Jewish customers and adhere to kosher religious laws. These establishments will basically not serve a hot meal on Friday night (unless it was cooked hours earlier and kept warm somehow) or on Saturday until nighttime. Restaurants that keep kosher close on Friday in the late afternoon (depending on the time of the year, around 3 or 4pm). Some will not open again until Sunday morning, but many open later in the evening on Saturday night after the Sabbath has ended, generally around 9pm, and then stay open later than usual.

Accommodations

There are several different types of accommodation options when traveling throughout Israel and the West Bank. Options range from five-star resorts to extremely casual accommodations, such as renting a room in someone's home.

GUESTHOUSES (ZIMMERS)

The fairly ubiquitous and lovely option of a *zimmer* (also spelled *tsimmer*) is one of the best ways to experience regional hospitality, food, and culture. A *zimmer* is typically family owned and operated and set up as a series of private cabins or bungalows spread across the *zimmer* grounds and centered around a main building where meals and sometimes recreation can be found.

There are two main categories of *zimmers:* luxury and luxury-rustic. The luxury-level *zimmers* include amenities such as a large, flat-screen TV and a whirlpool hot tub. The rustic *zimmers* usually won't include any kind of a TV and will emphasize a more natural, country experience. *Zimmer* cabins often have private porches, but ask in advance about bathing accommodations, because the bathtub (and sometimes the toilet) are often placed in a prominent spot in your room and not inside a closed-off bathroom.

Zimmers can be found throughout Israel. The website for **Rural Tourism in Israel** (www.zimmeril.com) is an invaluable resource, as many *zimmers* don't maintain their own website, social media pages, or even have an email address and can only be reached by telephone.

Some *zimmers* are located in moshavs, which are basically cooperative neighborhoods that are sometimes a bit off the beaten path.

GUEST ROOMS

Arranging for a guest room is a tricky matter, and you probably need to be in the country already or have a trusted go-between like a tour guide to make arrangements.

BUDGET, MID-RANGE, BOUTIQUE, AND HIGH-END HOTELS

The range of hotels in Israel and the West Bank is just as broad as any other region that caters to tourists, but the main thing to be aware of is the size of rooms, even in higher-end hotels, are often on the smaller side, more in accordance with European standards. Budget hotels and mid-range hotels will often be a bit sparse in the furnishings and will have tile floors (not carpeting), but they usually have free wireless Internet. High-end and luxury hotels, in turn, will usually charge for Internet access, but have every amenity you can imagine, down to the smallest detail.

There are a couple of common features for the majority of hotels in the region. One is that breakfast is included with the rate of your room. In some cases, you can upgrade your room rate to have all meals included. Once in a blue moon, the standard breakfast-included practice is not kept at a hotel, so it is always best to ask in advance.

The included breakfast is typically served around 7am-9am, but always ask in advance. It includes hot and cold drinks, salads, eggs, toast, and more. If you try to take food out of the breakfast area, hotel staff will charge you extra.

The general practice for room service in mid-range hotels and up is that you can often get at least hot and cold drinks delivered to your room.

HOSTELS

The hostel system in Israel is surprisingly well-developed and the best of the hostels book extremely far in advance, sometimes as far as six months. Hostel options in Jerusalem include places to stay in the Old City as well as near City Center. The **Israel Youth Hostel Association (IYHA)** (tel. 059/951-0511, www.iyha.org.il/eng) has English-speaking hotline representatives and a very easy-to-use booking website for hostels throughout the region. Though the hostel listing is not comprehensive, it includes hostels that are sanctioned members of the IYHA.

KIBBUTZIM

There are a number of kibbutzim in Israel that generate part of their economy from operating luxury, resort-like hotels or more mid-range accommodations. When you stay at one of these kibbutz hotels (Ramat Rachel on the outskirts of Jerusalem is a good example), you will typically have access to certain kibbutz amenities, including a swimming pool, playgrounds, and the like.

Conduct and Customs

The general rule with conduct and customs in Israel and the West Bank balances on two ends of the spectrum: live and let live or extremely strict. In general, the more religious the area you are in (Jewish, Muslim, or Christian), the more strictly the conservative conduct and religious customs are adhered to. This includes everything from clothing to food, and it particularly applies to women.

ETIQUETTE

There are a few things to keep in mind when navigating the general regional etiquette of the Middle East. One is that you will likely encounter at least one person who is unwilling to shake your hand for religious reasons, again, particularly if you are a woman.

Also in a general sense, people are more direct, less prone to affected pleasantries, and often more willing to get involved in other people's personal affairs (including giving unsolicited advice or directions). This directness and familiar approach to communicating takes some getting used to.

CONVERSATION

When talking with people, it is advisable to speak up and be as direct and decisive as possible. If you know what you want or what you are after in a conversation or interaction, you're likely to get better results than if you hesitate or are timid about what you're saying. Don't be alarmed or intimidated if someone speaks to you in a loud voice that sounds like yelling. It is just conversation.

In Israel, the common greeting is "shalom," which means peace. In Arabic, it is "as-salaam alaikum," which means peace be upon you. If you say nothing else in the native languages, try these two phrases out.

CLOTHING

Before you travel to any area, check in advance what the customs regarding clothing are. In the ultraorthodox areas of certain towns in Israel and in some towns in the West Bank, people dress extremely conservatively. It's not advisable to walk through these areas in shorts and a tank top on a hot summer day. In Jerusalem, there have been cases of women being accosted and even physically attacked for dressing in a manner that is considered immodest by the religious.

Religious Sites

Most religious sites have signage to explain the site's expectations. Depending on the site, this can include covering your head, taking off your hat, covering your shoulders, having covered legs, keeping your cell phone off, refraining from flash photography, refraining from photography completely, keeping your speaking voice low, no public displays of affection, and on and on.

DINING

When you go out to eat, you can stay as long as you want. It is the rare waiter who will approach you in any eating establishment to ask if you want the check, unless the restaurant is extremely busy. The custom is to let customers sit as long as they want until they are ready to leave. The waiter might continue to come back and ask if you want more of something, but they will not prompt you to leave.

The one exception to this is the preemptive measure some places will take during Shabbat if you come in without a reservation. The customary approach is to explain that you don't have a reservation, to which the host or hostess might say they have a table for you but it is reserved for a group that is arriving in a certain amount of time. That is your cue to understand that you can sit and eat, but you must leave within the allotted time.

COOKING OUT

In general, as with many other things in this region, the rules about cooking out are fairly loose. Basically, you can cook out almost anywhere you want to (within reason).

If you happen to be in Israel during the Yom Ha'atzmaut holiday (National Independence Day, around May 14, corresponding to the Jewish calendar), you will see cooking out like you have probably never witnessed. Most businesses shut down and people go out in droves to find any piece of ground they can to cook out on. Even the pristine grass on the grounds of the national rose garden next to the Israeli Knesset is fair game for setting up a small grill and starting a fire. If you pass by one of the large (or small) parks in any city, you will see a cloud of smoke hovering above it from the cookout frenzy.

If you want to take part, it is easy to buy a small grill (NIS20) prior to the holiday at most grocery stores and small convenience stores.

SHABBAT (SABBATH)

The Jewish Shabbat (or Sabbath) starts on Friday at sundown and ends on Saturday night after three stars are out in the sky (when it is fully dark). Depending on how religious someone is, Shabbat can involve restrictions on using motorized transport, electricity, and working. Taxicabs still operate, but their fees are higher than normal.

In Israel, Shabbat is the weekend for everyone (except Muslims and most Arabs) whether they are religious or not. All government offices and services stop, including public transportation. One exception to a major shutdown is East Jerusalem, which is predominately Arab, and where everything continues to hum along as normal. Arab areas shut down on Friday afternoon, which is their major prayer time during the week. Also, any restaurant that is kosher is closed. In Jerusalem, that means that all but about 15 restaurants shut down for more than 24 hours.

RAMADAN

The holy month of Ramadan is generally from early July to early August; the exact dates vary slightly every year. Ramadan involves fasting from morning until evening, when a large meal is eaten. It is the one time of the year during which it would be quite inconvenient to visit a predominately Arab area, as many things close or operate on a special schedule.

Travel Tips

WHEN TO GO

You will generally want to avoid traveling to Israel and the West Bank during major religious holidays. Jewish, Muslim, and Christian calendars are available online, but the biggest holidays are Passover and Easter, Hanukkah, Sukkot, Ramadan, and Christmas. Hotel rates will be higher during these times, and many venues will be closed in certain areas.

The month of August is not an advisable time to visit Jerusalem. It is a time of year when many children are not in camp, day care, or school, and it is also a major holiday for the ultraorthodox community. Jerusalem becomes extraordinarily crowded (including the museums, roads, and restaurants) during this time.

SHOPPING AND BARGAINING

There are a few unique aspects to shopping in the region. One is that there are numerous Israeli designers who design and make wonderful clothes, shoes, bags, and other accessories. These are unique, domestically produced items that are largely sold only in Israel. They are typically extremely well made, durable, and attractive. Made in Israel products are sold everywhere from large shopping malls to small boutique stores on the street.

One of the worst types of places to shop is in tourist areas. The prices, quality, and selection are often worse than elsewhere, and vendors will often try to convince you that something is antique or much more valuable than what they are selling it for. The upside, however, is that if you have the stamina, you can drive a pretty hard bargain with shopkeepers, particularly in Jerusalem's Old City shops. Shop owners might chase you after you start walking away in refusal of a price they offered, shouting out an even lower price. The general rule of thumb is not to expect to negotiate the price down by more than a third.

When buying antiquities of any kind, always get the certificate of authenticity from the seller, as grave robbers and antiquities thieves are a major regional problem. If an antique item you bought is discovered by customs, you will not be able to leave the country without a certificate from the seller.

If someone bought you a present while you are in the country, don't leave it wrapped; be prepared to have it scanned for bombing materials by the Israeli security personnel at the airport if you mention you are carrying a gift someone gave you.

TIPPING

It is customary to tip about 15 percent to service personnel, including waiters and bellhops, but it is not customary to tip taxi drivers. In restaurants, you will often see a note on your receipt which says Service is Not Included, which means that they want your money.

OPPORTUNITIES FOR STUDY AND EMPLOYMENT

There are many work and study opportunities in Israel, but unless you plan on staying long-term, most of the work opportunities are voluntary and unpaid. There are several types of programs that you can participate in, including internships and fellowships, touring and experiential activities, volunteering programs, Hebrew language programs, Arabic language programs, academic programs, Jewish studies programs, and activist-based travel (similar to volunteer experiences).

Israel is pretty well equipped for travelers with disabilities, but the older sections of cities, such as Jerusalem's Old City, are less so. The West Bank is not really set up to serve travelers with disabilities, though some of the nicer hotels do make certain accommodations.

TRAVELING WITH CHILDREN

Though it might seem like a tricky area to travel with children, nothing could be further from the truth. As long as adequate preparations are made for sun protection and hydration, it is very easy to travel in the region with a child. The general culture in this part of the world is centered on family life (including extended families), and people are accustomed to families that have at least 3-7 children.

For this reason, it is easy to be accommodated for your needs with children in hotels, restaurants, and in tourist destinations. One caveat to this is that the public safety standards are not as strict as North Americans are accustomed to, so it's best to be a bit more alert about what's going on around you. Most hotels will have very nice cribs (some charge a bit extra, but not all) that you can use in your hotel room. Ask for the crib in advance, and it will be set up in your room on arrival.

The general regional atmosphere in regard to children is accepting also in restaurants, where something like a crying baby likely won't cause any of the customers to even bat an eye. The typical sounds and actions of babies and children are so familiar in the culture that you can usually expect a very understanding and helpful reaction when traveling with children.

A young tourist examines souvenirs in Jerusalem's Old City market.

WOMEN TRAVELING ALONE

It can be a bit tricky for a woman to travel solo in certain parts of Israel and in the West Bank. The best way to keep a low profile is to dress conservatively. There aren't any real dangers for a woman traveling alone in this region, but it is also not that common, and it is a male-dominated society with widely varying expectations about the role women play.

SENIOR TRAVELERS

The most important thing for senior travelers to keep in mind while traveling in the region is to be cautious about the potential dangers of the Middle East sun. In the hottest summer months, it's advisable to conduct outdoor activities before 10:30am and after 3pm. When it's hottest, always drink plenty of water and wear a hat and sunscreen.

GAY AND LESBIAN TRAVELERS

In conservative Jerusalem, there are some gay bars and clubs, but in day-to-day life, gays and lesbians are very much under the radar. Jerusalem is a city where you will seldom see anybody, gay or straight, making public displays of affection.

Health and Safety

MEDICAL CARE IN ISRAEL

Israel's health care facilities are modern, world-class operations, and if you need medical service, you can go to one of its many hospitals. Dial 101 from any phone at any time if you have an emergency (most people speak English). Some cities also have pharmacies and drugstores that operate 24 hours a day.

VACCINATIONS

You do not need vaccinations to enter Israel, but it is best to travel with valid health insurance. You can get travel insurance for your trip, which will protect you in the case of any major mishaps.

DEHYDRATION AND HEATSTROKE

You will see signs posted from the Israeli Ministry of Health reminding people to drink water and to carry it with you and drink it regularly (even if you're not thirsty) to avoid dehydration and heatstroke. Tap water is perfectly safe to drink in all parts of Israel.

When hiking, always bring water, sunscreen, and a hat, even if you are accustomed to being in a warm climate. If you get dehydrated or get sunstroke, the symptoms might not appear until you are in a dangerous condition. Experienced hikers will tell you that if you are drinking enough water, you should be looking for a restroom about every 90 minutes or so.

BOMB SHELTERS AND ALARMS

Many houses, buildings, and hotels have bomb shelters. If you don't know where a bomb shelter is, the next safest place is in a stairwell as far from windows as possible.

The sound of a wailing bomb alarm is unmistakable and could go off at any time of day or night. From the time you hear the sound of the alarm, you will have about two minutes to get to a bomb shelter or safety before impact.

Israel's highly sophisticated Iron Dome system (partly funded by the U.S. government) has been tested plenty in recent years, and it is very effective at intercepting and detonating incoming rockets while they are still in the air. Most of them never hit the ground.

CONTACT LENSES AND GLASSES

If you wear contacts lenses or glasses, note your prescription level in advance, as you will be able to easily buy contacts or glasses in any drugstore, optometrist shop, or glasses store once you are in the country. There is no doctor's prescription required.

ESSENTIALS
HEALTH AND SAFETY

STRAY CATS

You might notice a large number of stray cats wandering around different cities, particularly in areas where there are more people. Most of these cats are not only strays, they were born on the streets and might carry disease. Don't pet stray cats or try to feed them.

Don't be tempted to pet or feed the stray cats.

MONEY

Israel

The Israeli currency is the New Israeli Shekel (NIS or shekel), and it is divided into 100 Agorot. The most current exchange rates are available from the **Bank of Israel** (tel. 02/655-2211, www.bankisrael.gov.il). The U.S. dollar generally hovers around an exchange rate US$1 to NIS4. Major tourist areas have currency exchange services.

Israeli banks are open Sunday-Thursday about 9am-noon, then close for a few hours, and open again about 2pm-5pm. Cash can be withdrawn from ATMs 24 hours a day.

Non-Israeli citizens can get a VAT (Value Added Tax) refund if they don't have an Israeli passport and are visiting Israel as a tourist. The goods should have been bought in a store included in the VAT refund program and the purchase amount in one tax invoice including VAT must exceed NIS400.

The West Bank

You can pay for goods and services in the West Bank using U.S. dollars or Israeli shekels, though it is best to use shekels.

Traveler's Checks and Credit Cards

It's possible to pay for goods and services with traveler's checks in Israel, but it might be a bit inconvenient. A good bet is to change traveler's checks to cash as needed. Major credit cards are accepted almost everywhere.

CONSULATES

Israel's designation of Jerusalem as its national capital is a matter of some dispute in the international arena. In diplomatic terms, this translates to foreign embassies being located in Tel Aviv and some foreign consulates being located in Jerusalem. Only some countries with an embassy in Tel Aviv also have a consulate in Jerusalem.

The **U.S. Consulate General** (18 Agron St. and 14 David Flusser Rd., tel. 02/622-7230, http://jerusalem.usconsulate.gov, jerusalemvisa@state.gov for non-immigrant visa questions) has two buildings. The one for consular services is located between the neighborhoods of German Colony and Bak'a and the Sherover-Haas Promenade.

The **U.K. Consulate General** (19 Nashashibi St. in Sheikh Jarrah, tel. 02/541-4100, http://ukinjerusalem.fco.gov.uk, britain.jerusalem@fco.gov.uk) is in East Jerusalem.

The **Embassy of Canada** (3/5 Nirim St., Tel Aviv, tel. 03/636-3300, www.canadainternational.gc.ca/israel, taviv@international.gc.ca) is in Tel Aviv. Canada does not maintain a consulate in Jerusalem.

The **Embassy of Australia** (Discount Bank Tower, Level 28, 23 Yehuda

Aviv. Australia does not maintain a consulate in Jerusalem.

COMMUNICATIONS AND MEDIA
Internet Access
One of the best features of Israel is the fact that you get free wireless Internet almost everywhere you go. Most restaurants, cafés, and coffee shops have free wireless Internet, so as long as you have a computer you can get Internet access. Internet cafés are much less common, but most large luxury hotels with business centers will agree to let you use their business center computers for a small fee.

Printed and Online News
There are several major newspapers in English, Arabic, Hebrew, and Russian that are distributed throughout Israel and the West Bank. Those published in English and Hebrew include the *Jerusalem Post, Ha'aretz,* and *Yedioth Ahronoth* (known online as Ynet), among others. The *International New York Times* is published only in English, and the *Jerusalem Report* is an English-only magazine sold in bookstores and on newsstands.

Arabic publications include *al-Sennara* and *al-Ittihad,* among others.

MAPS AND TOURIST INFORMATION
Maps
Israel's **Ministry of Tourism** (goisrael.com) has online maps of major cities and pilgrimage sites as PDF files that can be easily printed. **Eye on Israel** (www.eyeonisrael.com) has interactive maps of Israel and major cities, including tourist sites, hotels, geographical information, and a historical atlas. Hard copy maps, including city maps, road maps, touring maps, and hiking maps are available for online purchase on the Ministry of Housing and Construction's website (www.gov.il).

Tourism Offices
There are tourist offices located throughout Israel in major cities, including in **Tel Aviv** (Ben-Gurion International Airport, tel. 03/975-4260, doritk@ tourism.gov.il, open 24 hours a day) and **Jerusalem** (Jaffa Gate, tel. 02/628-0403, orenm@tourism.gov.il, 8:30am-5pm Sat.-Thurs., 8:30am-1pm Fri.).

WEIGHTS AND MEASURES
The Israeli system of weights and measures is based on the metric system. The most common conversions include 1 kilogram (2.2 pounds), 1 meter (1.1 yards), 1 liter (1 quart), 1 dunnam (0.22 acres), and 1 kilometer (about 0.6 miles).

ELECTRICITY
Similar to most European systems, Asia, and the Middle East in general, Israel uses a 220V system (220V-240V) at 50 Hz. European visitors

shouldn't have any trouble, except for a possible converter for the unique Israeli outlet system of a type H plug that has two flat prongs that form a V and one vertical grounding prong on the bottom. You can buy a converter for an American plug at any electronics store for about NIS4.

Visitors from the United States will need to make a few adjustments because they use 110V appliances, and also visitors need to be aware that Israel's 50 Hz system might cause some problems with appliances (such as analog clocks), even with a transformer. Don't plug your 110V directly into an Israeli outlet, and be careful with bringing a hair dryer from the United States.

TIME ZONES

Israel and the West Bank operate three hours ahead of Greenwich Mean Time (GMT+3). They also operate on daylight saving time; they switch to daylight saving time on the last Friday before April 2 and switch back on the last Sunday before Yom Kippur (about late Sept.-Oct.) every year.

Resources

Hebrew Phrasebook

PRONUNCIATION

Hebrew is, for the most part, a straightforward language that is logical and doesn't have very many exceptions.

Consonants

Aleph	Ah-lehf
Bet	BEHT
Gimel	GEE-mel
Dalet	DAH-let
Hey	Hay
Vav	Vahv
Zayin	ZAIN
Khet	het
Tet	TEHT
Yud	YOOD
Kaf	KAHF
Lamed	LAH-med
Mem	Mehm
Nun	NOON
Samech	Sah-Mekh
Ayin	Ah-yeen
Pe	PEH
Tsadi	SAH-di
Quf	KOOF
Resh	Rehsh
Shin	SHEEN
Tav	TAHV

Accent

Through the ages, as the Jewish population spread throughout the world, different accents developed. Most people who speak Hebrew today speak what is known as modern Hebrew, which is the Hebrew that is used in Israel. The variance in pronunciations is seen primarily during religious ceremonies, especially when reading from the Torah.

COMMON PHRASES

Hello, good-bye, or peace *Shalom*
Good morning *Boker tov*
Good evening *Erev tov*
See you soon *L'hitra'ot*
What's up? *Ma nishma?*
Yes *Ken*
No *Lo*
Thank you *Toda*
Excuse me/I'm sorry *Slicha*
Please/You're welcome *Bevakasha*
What is your name? (male/female) *Eich korim lecha/lach?*
My name is… *Shmi…*
How are you? (male/female) *Ma shlomcha/shlomech?*
Fine, OK *B'seder*
Not good *Lo tov*
Excellent *Metzuyan*
I'm tired (male/female) *Ani ayef/ayefa*

BASIC, COURTEOUS, AND RELIGIOUS EXPRESSIONS

Please excuse me *Slicha bevakasha*
Just a minute *Shneeyah*
Just hold on a minute *Shneeyah rega*
No thank you *Lo toda*

Thanks to God *Toda le-El*
Happy holiday *Hag sahmeah*

EATING AND SHOPPING

Do you have…? (male/female) *Yesh lecha/lach…?*
How much? *Kama zeh oleh?*
I want… (male/female) *Ani rotzeh/rotzah…*
I don't want… (male/female) *Ani lo rotzeh/rotzah…*
Money *Kesef*
Change (literally, "leftovers") *Odef*
Waiter/waitress *Meltzar/meltzarit* (though you will always just say *Slicha*)
Water *Mayim*
Coffee *Kafeh*
Latte *Kafeh Afuh*
Tea *Tay*

GETTING AROUND

I'm going to…(male/female) *Ani nose'a l'…/Ani nosa'at l'…*
There is… *Yesh…*
There is no… *Ain…*
Do you know where…is? (male/female) *Aht yoda'at eifoh nimtza…?/Ata yodea eifoh nimtza…?*
Wait/Just a moment *Rega*
Restaurant *Mis'adah*
Bathroom (services) *Sherutim*
Post office (mail) *Do'ar*
Street *Rechov*
Boulevard *Sderot*
Market *Shuk*
Museum *Muzion*
Synagogue *Beit knesset*
Church *Knaissia*
Central bus station *Tachana merkazit*
Taxi (regular) *Monit*
Shared taxi *Sherut*
Automobile *Mechonit*
Train *Rakevet*

Bus *Otoboos*
Hotel *Malon*
Hostel *Akhsaniya*
Room *Cheder*
Beach *Chof*
Grocery store *Makolet*
What is this?/What is the reason for this? *Mah zeh?*
Food *Okhel*
Right *Yemina*
Left *Smola*
Straight *Yashar*

AT THE BORDER AND AT CHECKPOINTS

Passport *Darkon*
Open (your trunk) *Leef to ach*
Are you American? *Ahtah Amerikai?*

EMERGENCIES

Do you speak English? (male/female) *Ata medaber Anglit?/Aaht medaberet Anglit?*
I don't speak Hebrew (male/female) *Ani lo medaber Ivrit/Ani lo medaberet Ivrit*
Police *Mishtara*
Doctor *Rofe*
Hospital *Beit cholim*
Passport *Darkon*

USEFUL QUESTIONS

Who *Mi*
What *Mah*
When *Matai*
Where *Eh-fo*
Why *Lama*
What is this? *Mah zeh?*
How *Eich*
How much does it cost? *Kamah zeh oleh?*
Where are the restrooms? *Eifo hasherutim?*

What time is it? *Mah hasha'ah?*
What happened? *Mah karah?*

NUMBERS

One *Achat*
Two *Shtayim*
Three *Shalosh*
Four *Arba*
Five *Chamesh*
Six *Shesh*
Seven *Sheva*
Eight *Shmone*
Nine *Tesha*
Ten *Eser*
Eleven *Achat esrey*
Twelve *Shtem esrey*
Thirteen *Shlosh esrey*
Fourteen *Arba esrey*
Fifteen *Chamesh esrey*
Sixteen *Shesh esrey*
Seventeen *Shva esrey*
Eighteen *Shmoneh esrey*
Nineteen *Tsha esrey*
Twenty *Esrim*
Thirty *Shloshim*
Forty *Arbaim*
Fifty *Chamishim*
Sixty *Shishim*
Seventy *Shivim*
Eighty *Shmonim*
Ninety *Tishim*
One hundred *Mea*

Two hundred *Mataim*
Three hundred *Shlosh meot*
Four hundred *Arba meot*
Five hundred *Chamesh meot*
Six hundred *Shesh meot*
Seven hundred *Shva meot*
Eight hundred *Shmone meot*
Nine hundred *Tsha meot*
One thousand *Elef*
Two thousand *Alpayeem*
Three thousand *Shloshet alafim*

DAYS OF THE WEEK

Sunday *Yom rishon*
Monday *Yom shenee*
Tuesday *Yom shlishi*
Wednesday *Yom revi'i*
Thursday *Yom chamishi*
Friday *Yom shishi*
Saturday (Sabbath) *Shabbat*

TIMES

Hour, time *Sha'a*
Day *Yom*
Week *Shavua*
Month *Chodesh*
Year *Shana*
Today *Ha'yom*
Yesterday *Etmol*
Tomorrow *Machar*

Arabic Phrasebook

BASIC PHRASES

Hello, nice to meet you *Marhaba ana saeed b-mareftak*
Do you speak English? *Hal tatakallam al ingliyziyya?*
Do you understand English? *Hal tafham al ingliyziyya?*
Yes *Na-am*
No *Laa*

I understand *Fahamt*
I do not understand *Laa afham*
Please repeat *Aiyd law samaht*
Good morning *Sabaah il-khair*
Good evening *Masa il-khair*
Good night *Tisibh ala khair*
Hello *Marhaba*
Hello (response) *Ahlan*
Goodbye *Ma-a is-salaama*

| How are you? (male/female) *Kayf haalak/haalik?* | Please speak more slowly *Laww samaht tahadith ala mahil* |

How are you? (male/female) *Kayf haalak/haalik?*

Fine *Bikhair*

Please speak more slowly *Laww samaht tahadith ala mahil*

Where is the bathroom? *Ayn il-hammaam?*

ASKING FOR HELP

I don't speak Arabic *Ana laa atahadith al-arabiya*

I'm sorry *Ana aasiff*

Suggested Reading

MODERN HISTORY AND CURRENT AFFAIRS

Carter, Jimmy. *Palestine: Peace Not Apartheid.* Simon and Schuster, 2006. A controversial look by former president Carter on how to bring peace to Israel and justice to Palestine.

Cohen, Rich. *Israel is Real: An Obsessive Quest to Understand the Jewish Nation and Its History.* Picador, 2009. An entertaining yet scholarly look at the history of the Jewish people from the time of the destruction of the Second Temple through the modern era.

Oz, Amos. *How to Cure a Fanatic.* Princeton University Press, 2010. Amos Oz is a beloved Israeli author and also internationally acclaimed. His pair of essays are about how to settle the question of real estate to bring peace to the Israeli-Palestinian relationship.

Senor, Dan, and Saul Singer. *Start-up Nation: The Story of Israel's Economic Miracle.* Twelve, 2009. A comprehensive and illuminating look at how Israel, a country of just over seven million people and limited resources, manages to produce more start-ups than more stable and well-developed countries like Japan, Canada, and the United Kingdom.

Zertal, Idith, and Akiva Eldar. *Lords of the Land: The War for Israel's Settlements in the Occupied Territories, 1967-2007.* Nation Books, 2009. The tragic yet gripping story of Jewish settlement in the West Bank and Gaza Strip and how it has impacted every facet of modern Israeli life, as told by a professor (Zertal) and a leading journalist (Eldar).

HISTORICAL CHRONICLES

Collins, Larry, and Dominique LaPierre. *O Jerusalem!* Simon and Schuster, 1972. The extremely thick book is an account of the bitter 1948 dispute between the Arabs and Jews over Jerusalem and emphasizes prominent individuals and the British in the process.

Flavius, Josephus, and William Whiston (translation). *The Wars of the Jews*. Digireads.com, 2010. One of the most frequently referenced historians of his time, Flavius Josephus was a Jewish historian and Roman citizen who wrote detailed (and some say questionable) accounts of the events of his time in AD 75.

Oren, Michael. *Six Days of War: June 1967 and the Making of the Modern Middle East*. Presidio Press/Random House, 2002. This international best-seller by the U.S. ambassador to Israel details six days of the definitive Arab-Israeli battle in June 1967 and its lingering impact on the peace process and the world.

LITERATURE

Grossman, David. *Someone to Run With*. Farrar, Straus and Giroux, 2000. The fictional story of life and love on the streets of Jerusalem, told from the perspective of a 16-year-old boy.

Oz, Amos. *Scenes from Village Life*. Houghton Mifflin Harcourt, 2011. A collection of essays set in a bygone era in a fictitious pioneer village.

FOOD AND TRAVEL

Ottolenghi, Yotam, and Sami Tamimi. *Jerusalem: A Cookbook*. Ten Speed Press, 2012. Jerusalem locals Ottolenghi and Tamimi explore the cuisine of their home city with its varied cultural and religious influences.

Saar, Jacob. *Israel National Trail and the Jerusalem Trail (Hike the Land of Israel)*. Gefen, 2011. A full guide to the Israel National Trail and the Jerusalem Trail and the hiking experiences they present, including maps and tips for the trail.

POLITICAL

Said, Edward. *Orientalism*. Vintage Books, 1979. From one of the region's most noted critics and authors comes an examination of how the West observes Arabs.

Shehadeh, Raja, and Penny Johnson. *Shifting Sands: The Unraveling of the Old Order in the Middle East*. Profile, 2015. A collection of essays edited by Shehadeh and Johnson about the shifting power paradigm in the Middle East.

THE HOLOCAUST

Range, Peter Ross. *1924: The Year That Made Hitler*. Hachette Book Group, 2016. The dark story of Hitler's life in the year 1924 and how it shaped the monster that he would become.

Safdie, Moshe. *Yad Vashem: Moshe Safdie—The Architecture of Memory*. Lars Mueller Publishers, 2006. Israel's most famous and prolific architect examines his painstakingly designed project: the Yad Vashem Holocaust memorial in Jerusalem.

Internet Resources

There are a good number of websites with useful information about Jerusalem and Israel in English. Some websites are slow to update or are missing information, so it's always a good idea to cross-reference information. The following is a selection of the best, most relevant, and most useful.

JERUSALEM

GoJerusalem.com
www.gojerusalem.com
A private venture dubbed simply GoJerusalem.com contains helpful, descriptive, and fairly up-to-date listings on hotels, tours, and sightseeing, though much of the information has been republished on iTravelJerusalem.

iTravelJerusalem
www.itraveljerusalem.com
The official tourism website of the city of Jerusalem was launched in 2012 and has current information on food, accommodations, sightseeing, and events.

The Municipality of the City of Jerusalem
www.jerusalem.muni.il
The Municipality of the City of Jerusalem website has basic information about the city and some resources for visitors.

GOVERNMENT

Israeli Government
www.gov.il
The Israeli government portal is a good jumping-off point for any branch of the Israeli government online.

Israeli Ministry of Foreign Affairs
www.mfa.gov.il
The official site for the Israeli Ministry of Foreign Affairs has domestic facts, issues, statistics, and foreign government relations information.

TOURISM AND CITIES

Eye on Israel
www.eyeonisrael.com
The private enterprise Eye on Israel offers interactive maps of Israel and its major cities, including tourist sites, hotels, geographical information, and a historical atlas.

Israeli Ministry of Tourism
www.goisrael.com
The official Israeli Ministry of Tourism website has online maps of major cities and pilgrimage sites as PDF files that can be easily printed.

PARKS AND RECREATION

Israel Nature and Parks Authority
www.parks.org.il
The official website of the Israel Nature and Parks Authority contains a comprehensive listing of the names, locations, admission fees, descriptions, and contact information for national parks and nature reserves throughout Israel (if you can get the spelling of the park right).

Israel National Trail
www.israelnationaltrail.com
A useful guide to the Israel National Trail, with maps, information, and guidelines to taking the hike.

Israel Youth Hostel Association (IYHA)
www.iyha.org.il/eng
The official website of the Israel Youth Hostel Association (IYHA) is easy to use and allows you to check the availability of youth hostels in Israel by region.

Zimmeril.com
www.zimmeril.com
Though not an official site for *zimmers,* this site has a fairly comprehensive listing of Israel's *zimmers* (guesthouses) throughout the country, including their contact information, which can be very hard to find otherwise.

Egged
www.egged.co.il/Eng
The official website of Israel's national bus company Egged, which also operates throughout Jerusalem, has route and ticket information, but you need to dig a bit to get the right bus number.

Israel Railways
www.rail.co.il/EN
The official website of Israel's national train system has convenient and easy to use listings of times and prices for rail tickets.

Jerusalem Light-Rail
www.citypass.co.il
Jerusalem's official light-rail website has schedule, ticketing, a route map, and news updates for passengers.

INDEX

List of Maps

Photo Credits

Also Available

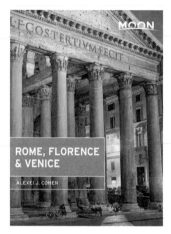

ROME, FLORENCE & VENICE
ALEXEI J. COHEN

TRIP OF A LIFETIME
ISTANBUL
& THE TURKISH COAST
LEEANN MURPHY

PRAGUE & BUDAPEST
TOM DIRLIS

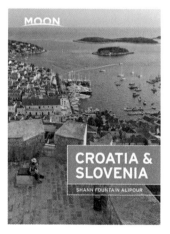

CROATIA & SLOVENIA
SHANN FOUNTAIN ALIPOUR

MAP SYMBOLS

- ~~~~~~~~ Expressway
- ::::::::: Primary Road
- ~~~~~~~~ Secondary Road
- - - - - - Unpaved Road
- · · · · · · Trail
- ·········· Ferry
- - - - - - Railroad
- ::::::::: Pedestrian Walkway
- ▭▭▭▭▭ Stairs

- ○ City/Town
- ◉ State Capital
- ◉ National Capital
- ★ Point of Interest
- • Accommodation
- ▾ Restaurant/Bar
- ▪ Other Location
- △ Campground

- ✈ Airport
- ✗ Airfield
- ▲ Mountain
- ✛ Unique Natural Feature
- Waterfall
- ♠ Park
- ⬛ Trailhead
- ⛷ Skiing Area

- ⛳ Golf Course
- Ⓟ Parking Area
- ⛰ Archaeological Site
- ⬥ Church
- Gas Station
- Glacier
- Mangrove
- Reef
- Swamp

CONVERSION TABLES

°C = (°F - 32) / 1.8
°F = (°C x 1.8) + 32
1 inch = 2.54 centimeters (cm)
1 foot = 0.304 meters (m)
1 yard = 0.914 meters
1 mile = 1.6093 kilometers (km)
1 km = 0.6214 miles
1 fathom = 1.8288 m
1 chain = 20.1168 m
1 furlong = 201.168 m
1 acre = 0.4047 hectares
1 sq km = 100 hectares
1 sq mile = 2.59 square km
1 ounce = 28.35 grams
1 pound = 0.4536 kilograms
1 short ton = 0.90718 metric ton
1 short ton = 2,000 pounds
1 long ton = 1.016 metric tons
1 long ton = 2,240 pounds
1 metric ton = 1,000 kilograms
1 quart = 0.94635 liters
1 US gallon = 3.7854 liters
1 Imperial gallon = 4.5459 liters
1 nautical mile = 1.852 km

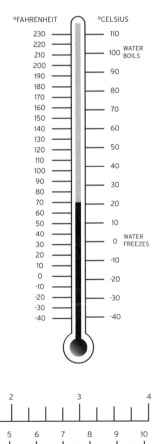

MOON JERUSALEM
Avalon Travel
An imprint of Perseus Books
A Hachette Book Group company
1700 Fourth Street
Berkeley, CA 94710, USA
www.moon.com

Editor and Series Manager: Kathryn Ettinger
Copy Editor: Ashley Benning
Graphics Coordinator: Elizabeth Jang
Production Coordinator: Elizabeth Jang
Cover Design: Faceout Studios, Charles Brock
Interior Design: Domini Dragoone
Moon Logo: Tim McGrath
Map Editor: Albert Angulo
Cartographers: Brian Shotwell, Albert Angulo, Stephanie Poulain
Indexer: Deana Shields

ISBN-13: 978-1-63121-659-6
ISSN: 2475-2886

Printing History
1st Edition — April 2017
5 4 3 2 1